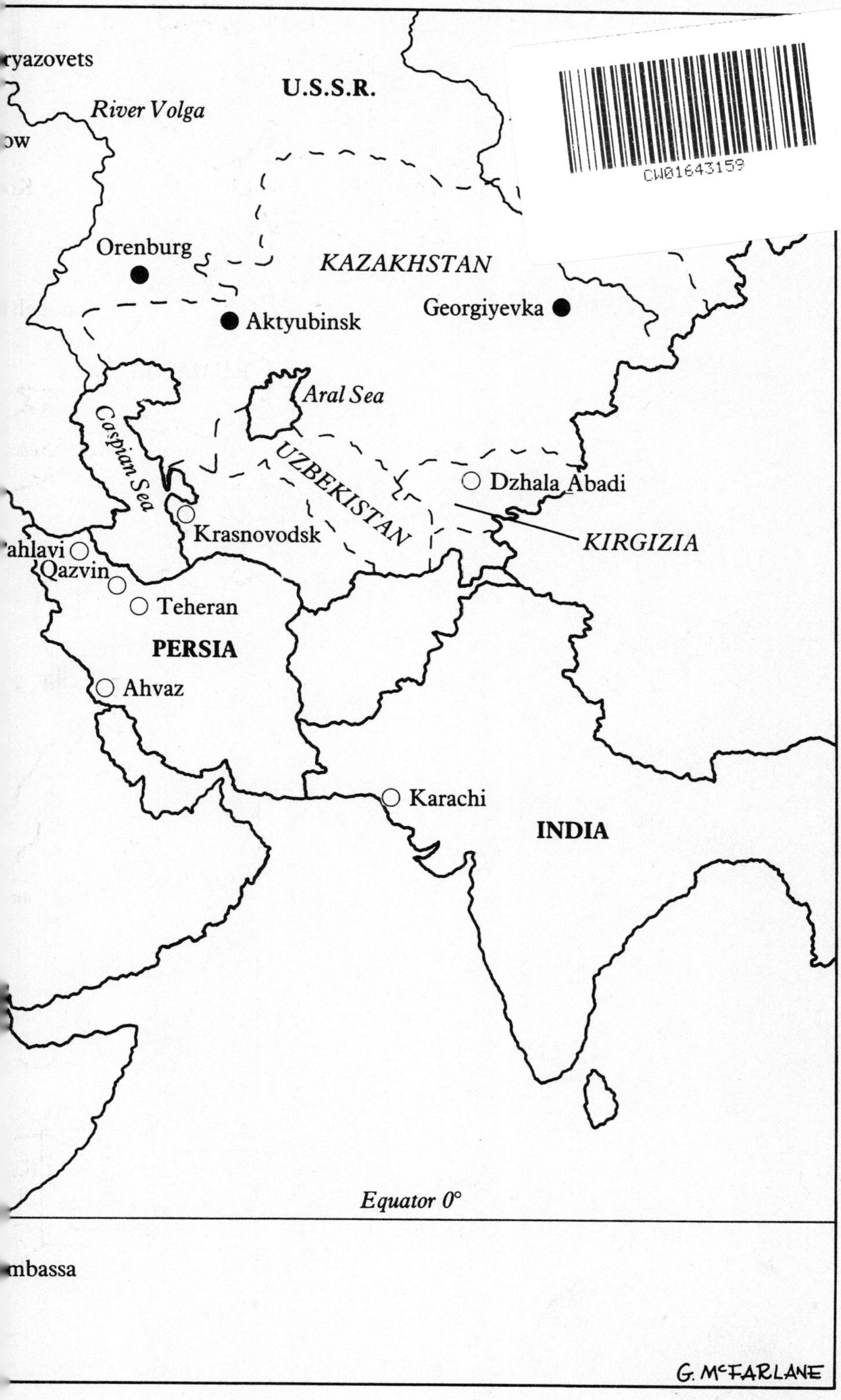
ryazovets
U.S.S.R.
River Volga
ow
Orenburg
KAZAKHSTAN
Aktyubinsk
Georgiyevka
Aral Sea
Caspian Sea
UZBEKISTAN
Dzhala Abadi
Krasnovodsk
KIRGIZIA
ahlavi
Qazvin
Teheran
PERSIA
Ahvaz
Karachi
INDIA
Equator 0°
mbassa
G. McFARLANE

FROM THE STEPPES TO THE SAVANNAH

Barbara Porajska

HAM PUBLISHING

Ham Publishing Company Ltd.
Ellan Vannin, Droghadfayle Park, Port Erin, Isle of Man.

British Library Cataloguing in Publication Data
Porajska, Barbara, *1929–*
From the Steppes to the Savannah.
1. Polish refugees, 1939–1948. Biographies
I. Title
325'.21'0924

ISBN 1-871235-30-8

Photoset in 11 on 12 point Plantin by Printagraphics Ltd., Onchan, Isle of Man.
Printed by Butler & Tanner Ltd., Frome and London.

To Katie and Robert

Acknowledgements

I am grateful to my good friend, Janet Nunn, for all her encouragement and advice while I was writing this book and to my daughter, Krysia, for accomplishing the tedious task of typing the manuscript.

Illustrations

between pages 56 and 57

Chapter 1

Although we spent many happy summers in an old wooden villa beside a large, beautiful lake, only one of them is etched clearly in my memory, as if it were only last summer. It is the summer of 1939. The very last, carefree summer of my childhood in my native Poland.

The weather is hot and dry. The woods around the villa are already beginning to change colour. Very slowly, majestically, autumn is approaching. For my sister and me it is a leisurely time for picnics in fields drenched with the fragrance of wild flowers, a time for lying in long, damp grass and gazing at the clear, blue sky or reading books which our mother would never allow us to read in her presence. My sister Ala is fourteen and I am almost ten years old. During the school year we are not exactly the best of friends. I am regarded as a silly child and a nuisance. She has her friends and often lets me know I am not one of them. When I am lonely and unwanted I usually console myself in the company of our dog Gogo. He is a wire-haired Dachshund, a very lovable and clever animal. I am convinced he knows how very important he is to me. When his big, brown eyes look at me mischievously, I forget my sorrows and we are ready to play. Away from school and her friends, my sister is very different. She treats me as her equal with whom she can share her thoughts and her forbidden books.

Like every year, this summer holiday is full of innocent fun. I am very happy with my friendly, caring sister, and Gogo, our constant companion, is a bundle of joy. Only one thing is different: our father is not with us. Mother told us that he is very busy and can't leave his post at present. Although he visits us at weekends he seems to be preoccupied by his own thoughts and spends hours talking quietly with mother.

The night is oppressively warm and very still. I can't sleep. I can hear my parents' talking. Their voices filter through the thin, wooden wall which separates my bedroom from the verandah, and fill me with dread. Father's restrained voice sounds very grave and urgent. "War is imminent, it is only a matter of days now!" I hear mother's despairing whisper; I think she is ready to cry. War, war, no one talks about anything else but war! I have a mental picture of fire, horses, confusion and people screaming. Just like a huge oil painting in father's study. The picture in a heavy gilded frame dominates the room and always compels me to look at it closely; faces twisted with pain, eyes full of fear, fallen bleeding horses, shining swords and in the background a red sky from the glare of fire. One can almost hear the terrified screams, feel the intensity of heat and smell the burning flesh. I pray this war is not going to be like that. Do I understand what war means? Am I frightened? My eyes are full of tears. Gogo senses that I am unhappy, rises from his comfortable position at the foot of my bed and snuggles close to my face on the wet pillow.

The next day I wake up late. Father is already gone. Thank goodness all the nonsense about war was only a dream! It is such a lovely day, one of those glorious days when the silvery-blue shimmering summer meets the golden autumn. Gogo is in the kitchen, he wags his tail begging for food. As soon as he sees me, he jumps up to greet me affectionately. Josephine, our maid, who accompanies us on all our summer holidays, is as usual busy getting breakfast. On the sun-drenched verandah mother, dressed in a travelling suit, sits by the table reading a newspaper. She seems disturbed. The breakfast in front of her has not been touched. A basket full of fresh crusty rolls and a small dish of homemade wild strawberry jam in the centre of the table looks very inviting, but I am not hungry. I am planning our day of fun. What shall we do today, my sister, Gogo and I? My thoughts are abruptly interrupted by mother's calm voice: "We are going back home today. We have to get gas masks and be taught how to use them, we have to get ready for war". Gas Masks?! My mental picture of war has no gas masks! I suppose this war is going to be different. We pack in a hurry and in silence. Gogo is very restless. I wonder, does he know? Chilling, odd pangs in my stomach tell me that this beautiful autumn day is going to be marred for ever. Soon my father's car, driven by his chauffeur, stops in front of our holiday villa. Father is not there. My uncle gets out of the car and helps to load the luggage. He is not in his usual jovial mood.

We all get in. I have Gogo in my arms. He cuddles up to me, I feel his small body trembling. We are driving fast. An uneven, bumpy road cuts through fields pregnant with ripe, golden corn. Suddenly we hear the piercing shriek of sirens. "It is only an air raid alarm test", my uncle says unconcerned. But almost immediately we hear aeroplanes above us and several shots. The car stops and we run out. "Down! Down on the ground!" my uncle shouts. Gogo jumps out of my arms. He is frightened. Silence. The plane is gone. The sky is bright blue and very calm. We get up, brushing dust and dry grass from our clothes. I look around for Gogo. He is lying peacefully in the golden, warm corn. A few red poppies grow nearby. They look like blood.

"Wait for me in the car," Uncle says in a stifled voice. Slowly he picks Gogo up and cradling him in his arms proceeds towards the nearest cottage. There he lays him gently outside the door, and when an old man answers his knocks, he exchanges a couple of sentences with him, gives him a few banknotes and walks away. Gogo is dead, yet I am not crying! How very strange. No one utters a word. We seem to be rooted in our car seats and benumbed. The car moves off. "Faster! Faster!" repeats my uncle.

We are back in Lvov. We have air raids every day. Every time the sirens sound we rush to the cellar. The only things we take with us are the gas masks. I hope we will never need to use them.

In spite of all the bombings our building has not been hit. In the cellar no one talks. It is dark and the cellar smells of damp and moulding apples. I can see rows of green shiny apples lying on a shelf lined with dry straw. I reach for one and take a large juicy bite; its bitter-sour taste calms me down. Mother sees me eating the unripe, unwashed apple, but she is not cross with me. Things must be very grave! We hear several explosions in the distance. The very last one is very near; the building shakes and I nearly choke on the last bite.

My aunt and her two children who live in the west of Poland, not far from the German border, are coming to stay with us. We on the east side are supposed to be safer. I am waiting for them with excitement. Roman her son is eighteen and Halinka her daughter is just thirteen years old. Roman is a very handsome boy. Every time he stays with us my sister's friends urgently need to see her after school to discuss some unfinished business. They stay for hours playing ping-pong with Roman in the playroom, talking and laughing. School matters are never mentioned. I hope they will not come this time because we will be very cramped in the cellar.

We hear some very bad news and mother is in a terrible state. The train on which they were travelling was hit by a bomb. Roman was killed instantly. My aunt is critically ill. Halinka was taken to a children's home and is being looked after by strangers. I am very sad. I see Gogo lying in the cornfield: he looks asleep. Does Roman look like that?

News of Roman's death spread quickly amongst Ala's friends. They start coming to see us and their sad long faces express genuine sorrow. They kiss mother, embrace Ala and nod to me. For a split second I can hear a ping-pong ball bouncing off the table, but the ping-pong room is empty. No music, no chatter, no laughter. Suddenly I am panic-stricken and have a strong feeling that from now on that's how it is going to be. The familiar shriek of sirens breaks this solemn gathering and we all run down to the cellar. The exploding bombs in the vicinity sound very ominous.

Chapter 2

We seldom see father now. I think the situation is very serious. A decision was made for mother and us to leave the country. The plan is to cross the Rumanian border. Unfortunately father is staying behind. He is the Chief Commissioner of the Police Force for Lvov and the province and he is needed at his post. For a while I forget about Roman. I am very agitated. I have never been abroad before.

We are packing a small suitcase, only a change of clothing for the three of us. I am astounded to see mother take some of her best gold jewellery. Surely there won't be any parties there. But Ala is very wise. "Just in case", she says. In case of what? Aren't we going away only for a couple of weeks, till things calm down a little? Father's composure and reassuring smile restores my confidence that very soon everything will be back to normal. He reminds us to brush our teeth after each meal and polish our shoes daily. Ala grins; clean teeth and shiny shoes are my father's obsessions. We throw our arms around his neck, a last kiss. He is standing at the gate waving, he even tries to smile. His large, light blue eyes are shining, he blinks several times. Oh God! I hope he is not going to cry! The car speeds through the partially bombed streets of our city. We see very few civilians. Mostly soldiers and firemen. Mother talks much more than is necessary and gesticulates in an excitable manner. She is worried about the canary we left behind, the potted plants, the dinner for father and the next week's shopping. We sit quietly in a corner of the car gazing at the ruins; she hasn't fooled us.

Late that evening we reach a small town a few kilometres from the Rumanian border. We decide to cross the border the next morning. A small white-washed cottage where we stop for the night is owned by a young couple with two children.

The husband is away at war. The young woman welcomes us warmly and we settle in for the night in a room which was previously occupied by her children. The night is still and peaceful. The unrest and chaos which war brings has not yet reached this corner of the country. Mother is more relaxed and we are all in a better frame of mind. I fall asleep thinking of father. I wake up confused. Where am I? It is still dark and the house is shaking. Two pictures on the opposite wall fall to the ground, broken glass scatters on the floor. What is this terrible roaring noise? I jump out of bed and look through the window which is facing the street. Tanks, big, heavy, dark green tanks are driving through the narrow streets of the town, and each has a red star painted on its iron body. I look at the moving mass of tanks almost hypnotised. I thought we were at war with Germany!

By now the whole house is awake. In the kitchen a young man in an airman's uniform is talking anxiously to mother and the young woman. I gather from the conversation that he has escaped from the Russians and very urgently would like to get rid of the uniform and the gun and put on civilian clothes. All this is arranged very swiftly. The man disappears through the back door and mother and the woman dig a big hole in the garden to bury the uniform and the gun.

All day the tanks roar through the empty streets. After the tanks there follow long columns of Red Army soldiers, marching, marching. After them a very large group of Polish soldiers and airmen. They are the first prisoners of war. The weary, down-hearted young men, many of them wounded, make a sorrowful and appalling sight. Two soldiers, one with his head covered in blood-stained bandages and the other dragging his injured leg, lag behind the rest. A Russian guard pushes them forcibly forward with the point of his gun. But they can't keep pace and one of them falls. We stand at the window watching, afraid to breathe. Ala bites her lips, I feel ashamed. Mother looks at us; she is very disturbed, her eyes are full of fear. I think she knows our thoughts. She puts her arms around our shoulders and says: "While we are concentrating on fighting the Germans, we are stabbed in the back by the Red Army. We have no chance, our position is hopeless." In spite of what she says I feel better, much better, and quickly compare this situation to something that happened at school not too long ago. My friend, a small but tough and brave girl, got into a fight with a bigger girl who used to bully her and make fun of her long, ginger hair. She was fighting fiercely defending her honour until another girl pushed her from the back. She fell down and broke her arm. My thoughts linger over that incident and I begin to hate the Germans and the Russians and I want to go home and see my father, as I am convinced that only father can overcome all the obstacles caused by the war.

It is obvious that we can't cross the border now. We are going back home by train. Although only yesterday I was looking forward to seeing a foreign country now I want to go back, as home is the only place where I shall feel safe. The station is in chaos. The trains are running late and they are packed with people and their belongings. I wonder where they are all going. The Russian troops are everywhere. While we wait for the train I think about how I can impress my friends back at school by telling them that I have seen the Russian soldiers, and they don't look like us at all. I think I will add that they have two heads and each head looks in a different direction. When after a long wait we finally board a train and get back to Lvov it is late at night. I find that the Red Army is already there, and I am very disappointed that I don't have a story to tell. I look around for father in a crowd of people but he is not at the station.

To get home from the station we catch the first available taxi and are stunned by the driver's stories told in a flat voice void of any emotion. To me, his callous report of the facts seems like a figment of his imagination. Yet looking at mother's pale and worried face I begin to believe that his tales are very likely to be true. "Just as well you were not in the city when the Red Army marched in. It was bad, very bad. Many civilians were killed. Nearly the entire police force was gunned down. Very few escaped, some were taken to prisons", the driver relates in a very matter-of-fact tone of voice. Mother looks ghostly pale, I fear she is going to faint. She rolls down the taxi's window and takes a deep breath of fresh air. Before we reach our destination she asks the driver to stop. We get out at the corner of a busy square, just a stone's throw from the street where we live. We can't go home. The whole vast building, which had been the Police

Headquarters for Lvov and the province, is surrounded by tanks, and soldiers are guarding the gates. In this building, barely a few days ago, we occupied a very spacious and comfortable apartment which adjoined father's offices. Now it is the Headquarters of the K.G.B. and our home is the residence of the top commander.

No one knows what happened to father. Mother decides to go to one of our friends, hoping that they are still there and the house has not been bombed. Thankfully they are well, but their once beautiful home has been divided into little flats to house homeless families. In spite of this there is also room for us. I can't help wondering why we are not staying with my other aunt and uncle who live in the same part of the city. One day I dared to ask mother and she firmly replied that we won't be going there even for a visit. My clever sister knows the reason. Apparently they are terrified to have any contact with us because of father's position in the police force. Now father and his family are the foremost enemies of the present régime. I must be honest to admit that I am very relieved, as the prospect of living there fills me with horror. Although they are not much older than my parents, they seem so ancient, so stiff and so very, very proper. Their gloomy home filled with expensive antiques and boring books looks like a museum in which one is not allowed to jump or sing or even be miserable. They have one daughter Alexandra and she is an example of perfection. This good news takes a load off my mind and, looking at Ala, I think she is just as pleased.

Chapter 3

At mother's friends' house we occupy one large bright room. We are quite comfortable. However, the atmosphere in the whole household is very tense.

The husband of mother's friend, a high-ranking police officer, is still living with his family, which is very surprising because, apart from the few lucky ones who escaped abroad, the entire police force was either shot or taken as prisoners, just as the taxi driver had told us, on the very first day that the Red Army occupied Eastern Poland. From the very beginning he has had to report daily to the Headquarters of the K.G.B. He goes there every morning for interrogations and cames back late in the afternoon. As the weeks go by he ages rapidly. His hair is getting grey, his face looks weary and pale and his sunken eyes are tired and full of fear. He never mentions what happens during his daily visits, and no one dares to ask. Every morning, before he leaves the house, he kisses and eagerly embraces his wife and two teenage sons, John and Mark. Every morning the dread of possibly never seeing them again shows on his despairing face. These daily goodbyes are heartbreaking. I for one feel like crying. This cruel, nerve-racking existence lasts for several weeks. One day the torment ends. We wait and wait, but he doesn't come back. We learned later that he was imprisoned and died soon afterwards. This very grave incident plays badly on my mind. One day, just before this tragedy, his older son, John, was teasing me. I was getting very annoyed and during our childish quarrel I shouted: "I bet your father is a spy!" I regretted it as soon as I said it. John jumped at me, his eyes full of anger. He grabbed me by my shoulders and shook me fiercely. "Never, never say that again!" he said in a muffled strange voice. I had a lot of trouble trying to explain to mother why I had such bad bruises on both my shoulders. She never did learn the truth.

I often think of our home and wish I could be in my cosy room full of my little treasures. Many times, unknown to mother, Ala and I wander in the direction of our house. We climb on a fence on the opposite side of the street and gaze at the windows of our house. When dusk falls upon the city and the lights are switched on inside, we can clearly see our old grandfather clock standing against the wall. "Look at its miserable face!" Ala comments one day. "Every time we see it the time is always the same. I bet they don't know how to wind it!" Actually she is right, it does look miserable. The hands of the clock stopped in such a position that they look like a mouth drooping down at the corners. I start giggling. "Even the clock doesn't like the company it is in" I say, highly amused.

I have never known mother to believe in the supernatural. On the contrary she used to sneer at those who believed in ghosts. But recently mother's friend, who practises spiritualism, persuaded her to attend a seance during which a medium communicates with a spirit. As Ala and I are very keen to see what goes on at such meetings, we pester mother to take us with her. We go there one evening. A room where eight people are assembled is situated in the attic. The room is large, but a low ceiling and a small window screened by a heavy dark curtain makes it very spooky. A solitary burning candle is all the lighting there is. A round table which stands in the middle of the room is marked at the edges with all the letters of the alphabet and the numbers from one to ten. We sit around it and, stretching our left arms, are asked by the medium to lightly touch a small plate which is placed in the very middle of the table. Curiosity mixed with excitement makes me feel quite feverish. Our faces look pale and tense as we are all expecting something extraordinary and slightly hair-raising. The medium calls the spirit of one woman's husband who was killed on the first day of the war. I am waiting to hear the man's voice or see his spirit in the form of a foggy mist. Nothing like that happens. However, the plate starts gliding smoothly in the direction of various letters, spelling out: "I miss you". An old man who is sitting next to me wants to know how his dead daughter is. Once again the plate spells out: "I am well". Through the medium's quiet voice mother asks if father is alive and the answer is: "Yes". Opposite me sits a very frail old woman; she looks awe-struck. Her whole family, including four grandchildren, were killed during the bombing of the city. Miraculously she escaped. Before she has a chance to let the medium know her wish she starts fidgeting, her breathing becomes fast and she faints. Someone puts the light on. The seance is over. Once back at home and in our familiar surroundings Ala and I start to feel very cynical about the entire performance. Ala is convinced that someone was pushing the plate. Mother, who is listening to our conversation, doesn't join in. I look at mother and Ala and feel very confused indeed. A week after the encounter with the spirits we hear from reliable sources that father is in fact alive and is a prisoner of war somewhere in Russia. This most joyous of news coincides with my tenth birthday and is the best present I could ever have.

We have been told that just before the Russians occupied Lvov, father gave a lot of our valuables to friends for safe-keeping. Unfortunately we can't trace any of them. The good news is that Josephine, our live-in home help, took a lot of our clothes, bed linen, kitchen utensils and cutlery. Nice, kind Josephine. She is keeping our belongings hoping that soon she will be able to return them to us. I urge mother to find her. Reluctantly mother agrees. After many enquiries we are set to go. Josephine is living in the industrial part of the city. The nearer we get to her home the more nervous and uneasy mother becomes. We climb some dark and dirty stairs; the door to Josephine's room is half open, she is resting on a partially-made bed. I rush forward to embrace her, but she looks at me with surprise and resentment. I take a step back and a friendly smile freezes on my face. She greets mother with coldness and expresses sorrow at father's fate. She is very sorry but she can't help us, as she doesn't know what happened to our belongings. I can't believe it. Our friendly Josephine, the girl with whom Ala and I spent many happy hours, the girl who taught me how to make the finest homemade vermicelli and delicate, crispy meringues, now doesn't want to know us. I look around. Josephine is wearing mother's blue dressing gown. The bedspread and bed linen is ours. I am just about to tell her so, but at that very moment a young Russian soldier walks into the room. Mother bids her a quick goodbye and we run down the stairs in silence. I am fuming. Ala tries to calm me down and, being very philosophical, points out that life is much more important than material things. But I think that in truth, life without material things is very miserable. And why, oh why has Josephine changed so much?

Since our risky and fruitless venture to see Josephine, mother is very uptight. "We should have never gone to see her, we were tempting fate!" she says. I think mother is overreacting and is making an unnecessary fuss. Ala and I try to calm her down, but she proceeds to tell us what is really going on: "Firstly, don't talk to strangers, and on no account tell them what your father's occupation was, as the families of policemen are maliciously persecuted. Secondly, and this I say with great sorrow, don't trust people, especially Ukrainians, who now collaborate with the Russians and would do anything to save their own skin. People like us are in great danger now. Only yesterday I heard the most outrageous story. Our friends, whom you remember as we visited them many times in their country house, are all dead. The majority of their farm workers were Ukrainians and, as soon as the Russians took over that part of the country, without any just cause, they turned against them, killing the whole family with scythes and axes, including a pregnant friend who was staying with them. They ransacked the house and burned it down to the ground. This is only one example of the atrocities which continually go on." She pauses for a while. "To tell you the truth, I am surprised we are still alive" she adds, her voice a whisper.

Chapter 4

We have had a very long break from school and mother decides that the time has come to resume our education. I am not very keen to go, but I am beginning to feel excited at the prospect of seeing my friends and teachers again. Our private school, the Convent of Sacre Coeur, has changed beyond recognition. The convent's beautiful chapel is closed. All holy pictures and statues of Jesus and Mary are gone. In their places hang portraits in ugly frames of Lenin and Stalin, red paper flowers and red paper ribbons. The Russian language is compulsory and Polish is forbidden. It is nice to meet all my old friends, but my two best friends are not there. No one knows what happened to them. It is just as well that we don't have to wear school uniforms, as we don't have any. We all take advantage of the lack of discipline. Every morning on the way to school, as soon as we turn the corner, Ala lets her hair down and tucks her belt in to make her skirt a little shorter. I follow her example, but I must admit that her legs are much slimmer and her long dark hair is nicer than mine. Often John catches up with us and we walk together part of the way. I think they like each other very much. I am so glad that John forgave me for that silly, nasty remark I made about his poor father.

Today is the anniversary of the Russian revolution. Our school is drenched in red. Flags, flowers, ribbons, everything is red, and we even have more huge portraits! We assemble in a big hall and are made to wave flags and sing Russian patriotic songs, praising Russian heroes. There are speeches and recitations. To crown it all, at the very end of the celebrations a shower of sweets drops on us from the ceiling. Sweets are everywhere, on the floor, on the chairs and on our heads. We hear someone's voice through a loudspeaker: "These sweets are from father Stalin who loves and cares for children. He is better and far more powerful than your God. When you sing holy songs praising God, sweets don't fall from heaven. So children rejoice and praise your father Stalin." Some children eat the sweets, but the majority just stand, not touching any of them. A lot of children are laughing. I feel sick.

Winter comes early. It has already snowed several times. Mother takes a lot of money from our savings to buy us some warm clothing. All our winter clothes were left behind the day we left for Rumania. A lot of shops are closed; those which are open have a very limited selection. We buy some jumpers, skirts, coats and shoes. The coats are too long and are in a horrible brownish colour, and the shoes are too big. We don't like them, but mother insists. "God knows when we will be able to get new coats and shoes, and you are still both growing. We have to be practical." I think of my smart blue coat lined with fur and I see it hanging in Josephine's wardrobe.

After each shopping session I feel very depressed. The town looks so dreary and dark. Gloomy people with worried faces rush through dirty streets, minding their own business. No one stops for a chat. We all seem to be afraid to talk. Lvov, once known for its friendliness and gaiety, has changed beyond recognition. The dark cloud of an unknown, uncertain future hangs over the city.

Very long queues form in front of the butchers' and grocers' shops. There is a shortage of everything. As the weeks go by the situation worsens. No meat, no sugar, no dairy products. Mother queues for hours to buy large quantities of bread, dry beans and peas. She cuts the bread into thin slices and dries it in the oven. When they are dry and cold she puts them into a big bag. We already have two large sacks of dried bread. "This is for the dark hours" she says. What does she mean, 'dark hours'? Isn't it dark enough now? What else can go wrong? We have no home, no father, Roman is dead, Gogo is dead, and the progressively worrying news of people being beaten and tortured by the Germans and the Russians increases our fear for father's safety. Surely it can only get better. How very wrong I am!

We hear rumours that very soon the Polish currency (the zloty) will cease to exist. Mother takes more money our from our savings and tries to buy whatever she can, but there is hardly anything left. The shops are bare. The black market is rife.

Rumours become reality. The Russian rouble is the legal currency now. All the money which people had in banks and saving societies is useless. I believe we lost a lot of money. To make matters worse, the winter is very severe. In spite of the cold weather mother often starts queuing for food very early in the morning, well before we go to school. After school we look for mother in queues outside the shops in our district. Once we find her, we take her place in the queue and she goes home to warm up and have something to eat. She tells us firmly to keep our place and not to let others push us away. When we get what we were queuing for we come home victorious and happy. But often, after several hours of queuing in the freezing weather, just when we are about to be served, we are told: "Sorry, everything is gone", and we feel miserable and very, very cold.

By some remarkable stroke of luck mother obtained some sugar and eggs on the black market just in time for Christmas and she is baking a cake. A delicious, sweet aroma lingers in the room and tickles my nostrils. I am sitting by a partially frost-covered window watching the falling snow. Tiny, crisp snowflakes flicker in front of my tired eyes. Street lights throw bright, glittering patches on the icy, slippery road. I feel lazy and sleepy, my heavy eyelids are slowly closing. I am dreaming of our last Christmas Eve.

My mother, Ala and I were in our big, warm kitchen in our home. Mother, dressed in one of her smart dresses, was putting the final touches to supper, which was ready and being kept warm on a hot stove. Ala and I, washed and with hair combed, were by her side. Josephine had gone home for Christmas. We were very excited but didn't dare to talk or laugh in case we missed the delicate, high-pitched tone of a bell. It was dark outside and the first star had appeared in the sky. The bell should ring any minute. The tension was unbearable. Then it rang! A clear, subtle, cheerful sound. We all rushed into the living-room. The room was in darkness. In the corner a tall Christmas tree stood, alight and glittering. Several red candles were burning, glass balls sparkled in a rainbow of colours. Father stood at the side of the tree. He was happy, his large blue eyes smiling. In one hand he held a small crystal bell which he was trying to hide. The sound of the bell had been the announcement that the angels had brought the tree and the presents. We pretended not to notice the bell, and at that very moment I really believed in angels. For a few moments we just stood there staring at the tree. It looked so beautiful! We said a short prayer and sung a couple of carols. I started fidgeting. Several presents wrapped in colourful paper were lying under the tree and were distracting my attention. I was very anxious to unwrap them. Gogo strolled into the room, sniffed the tree and pulled off one of the sweets which was hanging on a low branch. We all laughed. "Supper is ready", mother said.

The large round table in the dining room was covered with a snow-white tablecloth. A handful of hay placed under the cloth in the centre of the table was a reminder that Jesus was born in a stable. The table was laid with our best china and silver. There were five place settings. The fifth remained empty. A long time ago, when I was just a baby, my eldest sister Jadzia died, and ever since, once a year on Christmas Eve, mother set an extra place. Before we sat down, mother picked up a small plate with a piece of blessed rice-paper on it. We broke it into tiny pieces and each ate a piece, wishing each other health and prosperity, and we kissed and cuddled. After this very short but, for mother, always emotional ceremony, we sat down and began a delicious feast. No meat, this was the custom.

First, clear red beetroot soup with very tiny pasties filled with mushrooms, called uszka (ears), and cooked in the soup. Then, a variety of fish dishes: fish in horseradish sauce, fried fish with drops of lemon juice. After the fish course, another kind of pasty was served, this time with a potato and cheese or cabbage and mushroom filling and coated with melted butter. There was also a dish full of wide home-made noodles mixed with honey and poppy seeds. We were very full by then but there were still mouth-watering desserts awaiting us; cakes, jellies and cream tarts. Suddenly I hear mother's voice: "Barbara, wake up! The cake is ready and it looks really good!"

Chapter 5

Nineteen forty, the new year of the unknown.

I am only four months older since the beginning of the war, but I am not a child any more. My carefree world has changed completely. Ala and I are much closer now. We sleep together in one large double bed, together we freeze in long, endless queues, and during the dark winter evenings we talk. In our youthful imagination we create a brighter future, not realizing how hopeless the situation is. Mother, who before the war was always calm and cheerful, is now a bundle of nerves, but today she is in a very good mood. "Really good friends still exist", she says as she takes out her beautiful Persian lamb fur coat from her wardrobe. Apparently one of my parents' friends, with whom father had left some of our belongings, traced us and brought back mother's coat and two luxurious quilts, filled with the best camel's wool. I gently stroke the black, tight curls of the fur and snuggle my face in the silky warmth of the quilts. I close my eyes for a few seconds and see myself and Gogo jumping up and down, up and down on my parents' bed. "Get off the bed at once. Your shoes and Gogo's sharp claws will ruin the quilt", mother says sternly. I open my eyes; the marks where the long, silk threads were pulled from the cover are clearly visible. As winter is very severe, mother now wears her fur coat every time she leaves the house, but she puts an old, large raincoat over it to cover it completely. It would be dangerous nowaways to be seen in a fur coat which once belonged to a much better and more prosperous era. Those who were well off are now the enemies of the Russian people.

Again we hear very grave and terrifying news. On the 10th of February several thousands of Poles, mostly from the countryside, were deported to the Soviet Union. Destination: Siberia, Kazakhstan, Uzbekistan.

In long, gloomy queues we hear the unbelievable stories told in whispers. Stories of the old and sick being pushed into cattle trains and taken thousands of miles away. Stories of young boys who tried to escape, but when caught were put on different trains and separated from their families for ever, perhaps taken to prisons. Those who tried to resist were shot. We live in constant fear, uncertain what the next day will bring. Mother is very worried, she spends sleepless nights twisting and turning. In the morning she gets up tired, but rushes out to queue for food. She dries more bread. I begin to understand what she meant by "the dark hours". They are fast approaching. All her jewellery, which with foresight she took with her at the start of the war, she now, with Ala's help, very ingeniously sews into the quilts. Apart from jewellery she also hides in the quilts several gold coins.

Winter is losing its grip. We long for spring and warmer weather. But spring opens a new, horrific chapter in our lives.

Loud, impatient banging on the front door awakes the whole house. It is still dark outside. Noisy, rough voices of Russian soldiers mingle with the growl of lorry engines and reach us through a partly open window. Someone opens the door. The K.G.B. men and the soldiers, four, six, eight, ten soldiers, with rifles ready to shoot, walk into the house. They take their positions at each window and each door. Even the toilet is guarded, just in case someone tries to escape.

Our turn has come. It is the 13th of April. Mother in a confused state throws at us several pairs of underwear and clothing. "Put it on, put it all on!" she cries. "We might not be allowed to take any luggage!" I struggle with a third jumper, it is getting very tight and uncomfortable. I manage to put on four pairs of socks, thanks to the shoes which were bought too big. Ala gets hold of the precious quilts but one soldier grabs them from her saying that they are too bulky. Mother pales and with forced calmness begs him to be allowed to take them. "I would rather leave behind some of our clothes, but please may we take the quilts!" she says. The soldier reluctantly agrees and repeats that we can only take very little luggage. Mother's nerves are breaking down. She shakes and bursts into tears. She runs aimlessly around the room, she picks things up and drops them down. I am horrified to see that one soldier takes our bags of dry beans, peas and bread and throws them through the open window. They scatter onto the street below. The end of our provisions for "the dark hours!". Mother's fur coat provokes angry and sarcastic remarks. "The bourgeois are finished now", one of them says. A deliberate movement of his hand across his throat clearly demonstrates what kind of finish he has in mind. "There is no need to cry, you are going to join your husband", they say, sniggering. We know that this is a stupid and untrue remark. They hurry us, pointing the rifles. I run to the toilet and have to use it with the door open and the soldier looking at me. Three pairs of my pants get tangled up. With unsteady, shaking hands I pull them up. Just before we leave the room, one soldier picks up the kettle and hands it to mother. "Take it for 'Kipiatok'", he says. 'Kipiatok' means boiling water. Holding our bags in front of us, slowly we descend the stairs; in front of us mother's friend, John, Mark and the rest of the occupants of the house. John turns his head and looks tenderly at Ala.

The whole street is blocked by parked army lorries. Some, crammed with people, are already leaving. It seems that the entire street is being deported. In the dim light of a street lamp we look around for the boys and their mother but we can't see them. There is chaos and confusion. Soldiers are trying to restore some order by shouting and pointing the rifles at the sobbing, groaning people. Ala, very composed up till now, starts wailing hysterically; she swears and shouts in Russian. I am astonished to hear how many Russian swear-words she knows. Mother takes her by her arms and shakes her violently. "Stop it! You will be put on a different lorry and we might be separated for ever, so stop it!" she yells. Ala calms down and stares at us with wet, shiny eyes. Once on the lorry no one talks, the silence is bewildering. The station is crowded with thousands of people. Half of the population of Lvov is being taken away. Several goods and cattle trains are waiting in readiness. One by one the carriages are being filled with people; the very young and very old, ill and disabled. The confused, disorderly crowd pushes from all directions. Ala and I firmly grip mother's arms. A panic that we might be separated almost chokes me. The most important issue now is to stay together; it is a matter of life and death. Eventually we are thrust into an empty carriage together with a group of strangers. I see mother relax, she even smiles. "We have made it", she says, embracing us with her arms.

Day is breaking but the carriage is dark inside. There are only four very tiny windows, high up near the roof of the carriage, and thick iron bars run across them. The middle of the carriage is empty, but the two ends are filled with makeshift wooden benches, one very low and the second about a metre higher. I quickly climb on the upper bench which is near a tiny window. Mother and Ala climb after me. Older people seem to prefer the lower benches which are in complete darkness but easy to get to. We are terribly crowded; there must be forty or more of us. We are packed like sardines in a tin. Everybody holds on tightly to their pathetic belongings. Mother spreads the quilt on the hard bench to make it a little more comfortable. I am very intrigued by a large, round hole in the floor in a corner of the carriage, through which I can see railroad tracks. "That is our toilet", mother says. I look at her in disbelief. This can't be true! How can anyone use it in front of forty people? I am very determined not to use it and I tell mother so. But to my horror, I am told that most probably we won't be allowed to leave the carriage at any time during our journey. This news troubles me dreadfully. As time progresses we all become restless; it is obvious the hole has to be used. One young woman very cleverly hangs an old sheet around it. The problem is partially resolved. The sheet gives some privacy. With childish curiosity I wait for the first person to use it, and I soon see an old, sick man, supported by his wife, disappear behind the makeshift curtain.

The long train stands for hours at the station. The lorries, full of people, are still arriving at the station. I look through the tiny window, holding onto the iron bars. At last the train is full. Slowly it starts to move, creaking and shaking, faster and faster. We are leaving Lvov behind. In the distance I can clearly see church steeples outlined in the blue, cloudless sky. It is going to be a lovely spring day.

I am beginning to get accustomed to the dim light inside the carriage, and can distinctly see all forty people with whom we are sharing this prison on wheels. On our bench apart from us are five women and two young children. One woman is so fat that this really worries me. “She takes up so much room!” I moan to Ala. Every time the woman moves the wooden bench squeaks. I am very thankful that we are not on the bottom bench as I am almost sure that before our journey is over the bench will collapse and crush the people beneath. I share my thoughts with Ala and we both laugh. But our subdued giggles hide our real feelings. The two small children are about two and three years old and they crawl all over us. Mother is very tired and desperately wants to sleep but, every time she closes her eyes, little feet tread over her. There are some more women and children on the bench below. A tiny baby is crying non-stop; he is hungry, tired and cold. His very young mother, not much older than Ala I think, hugs him to her breast so possessively as if she is afraid that someone will snatch him from her. On the benches opposite us, apart from women and two teenage girls, are two middle-aged men and three very old couples. One man looks very ill and frail. He fidgets on the hard bench trying to find a comfortable position. I feel very sorry for him. His wife, a kind-looking old lady, folds the only blanket they have and puts it under his tired head.

We have only been in the carriage for a few hours and already two women opposite us are arguing over the bench space. They are pushing each other with their elbows and their irritable voices are getting louder. My quick calculations tell me that only about half a metre of bench space is allocated for each adult and small children are squeezed in between. Listening to the quarrel I wonder if they will ever be able to resolve the problem, as one woman is much fatter and her ample hips spread well beyond her rightful area. However, after a while, the slimmer woman gives up the fight. Slowly she turns her back on her opponent, who very promptly wriggles her fat bottom, pinning her to the carriage wall. “How many hours will we be in this train?” I ask mother. “Hours? It will be more like weeks!” mother replies. “For God’s sake, keep the baby quiet! I have a splitting headache!” someone yells from the bench below.

Chapter 6

The train speeds through the countryside. "We have just crossed the Polish–Russian border!" someone shouts. Then sudden silence. We can hear only the monotonous rattle of the train. The apprehension grows. Several people are making the sign of the cross, some are starting to pray. In our hearts we are all praying.

The very first day is nearing its end. We are hungry and thirsty. Some people have bread, some have apples or cheese. Mother has a small bag of sugar cubes. We share it with those who have nothing. All forty of us are beginning to get very worried, we have not been given anything to eat or drink yet, and what we have will last only a very short time. We don't talk; there is nothing to say. We settle down to sleep on our empty stomachs. I am very restless and uncomfortable. My shoulder aches. I think I am lying on mother's big brooch which is hidden in the quilt. With great difficulty I turn onto my other side, hoping that the fat woman on our bench will slim down soon. The tiny baby on the lower bench has not stopped crying.

The sudden jerk of the train wakes us up. The train has stopped. It is pitch black. Mother lights a couple of candles. I am amazed to see how many very important little items she has taken with her; that bag of hers is full of tricks! Someone looks at a watch: it is midnight. We hear loud voices and the squeak of the heavy carriage door. Two soldiers walk in and put down a couple of large, steaming buckets in the middle of the floor. "It is meal time", we are informed. So, after all, we are going to get fed! The soup is hot, grayish-looking and very watery. A few pieces of overcooked noodles float in it. It tastes terrible. I am trying to convince mother that I am not hungry, but she insists, adding that I should stop being so fussy as it is all we are going to get. Two people from each carriage, closely guarded by soldiers, are allowed to go out and get some boiling water. One old man emerges from his dark corner on the bottom bench carrying a large steel flask; the flickering candle-light makes it shine. "Hold it!" we hear the soldiers shout. Rifles are pointing at all of us. We freeze. What is happening? At once the carriage is surrounded by soldiers. An officer walks into the carriage, the rifles in readiness. He points at the flask in the man's hand. "Bomb", he says. "Bomb!" I start giggling. Ala nudges me with her elbow. In spite of being frightened we can't stop laughing. The old man, with a bewildered look on his face, explains that this is only a water container and demonstrates it by opening the top. The soldiers relax, the rifles are lowered. A sudden draught from the open door blows the candle flame out. "I wish I could see their stupid faces!" I say to Ala. The next night Ala and another young girl go out to get the boiling water. They take with them two kettles and four pots; it is as much as they can manage to carry. In addition Ala puts two large, empty bottles into her pockets. They come back after about half an hour and, once the water is distributed amongst our fellow travellers, Ala scrambles up onto the bench. She looks flushed and excited. "I talked to John for a brief moment", she whispers. "They are somewhere at the very front of the train, and John is planning to escape! He wants me to come with him!" "For God's sake, don't be so stupid!" I gasp. "I am not only going to tell mother about your ridiculous idea, but the soldiers as well!" I whisper back, meaning every word I say. Ala looks at me strangely and knows that I am not joking. After this exchange of thoughts we ignore each other till the next morning. The narrow beams of bright, spring sunlight, which filter through the barred windows, wake us up very early. Ala pouts her lips, turns her back on me and, staring at the tiny square of clear, blue sky, informs me that she has changed her mind. But I don't trust Ala and watch her closely. Thank goodness the expeditions to fetch the boiling water are taken in turns; this is very consoling. By the time her turn comes again, we will be thousands of miles away from the Polish border and a hazardous escape would be quite pointless. The feeding routine is always the same, we are only fed at night. We wait till we are given the soup and then we settle down for the night. The soup is always very insipid and varies little. Sometimes, instead of noodles, barley floats in it. The worst of all is the fish soup. Afterwards the entire carriage smells of fish for hours.

Four days have passed. Today I feel exceptionally hungry and am waiting impatiently for our meal time. Darkness is falling and in about three hours the train should stop. Two people in our carriage are getting ready to go out to fetch the boiling water. This short expedition is one thing we all look forward to. To be able to stretch our stiff, aching legs and breath fresh air is all we wish for at present. Today the lucky ones are the fat woman from our bench and the single, middle-aged man from the opposite bench. The man puts on his long coat and stuffs his pockets with various little objects which he usually keeps by his side in a small leather bag. Though a candle flame, which feebly flickers in one corner of the carriage, gives very little light, I can see that his hands are trembling and the pale face is strikingly tense. The train stops sooner than I expected. Through the tiny window I see half a dozen small, grim-looking buildings and just beyond them a forest which in the shadow of the night looks like a very dark, dense mass stretching far beyond my scope of vision. I see people with pots, pans, bottles and kettles. One woman, apart from carrying two small pails, has three rubber hot-water bottles tied to a belt around her waist. I am amazed at her ingenuity. The people form an orderly line and start queuing patiently for the water which is being distributed from one of the buildings. Watchful soldiers walk up and down the line. Nothing new, I have seen it several times before. The pair from our carriage mingle with the rest of the small crowd and disappear from my sight. Two buckets of hot steaming soup, placed by the soldiers in the centre of the carriage, smell revolting. Fish soup again. But I am very hungry and tonight I am determined to eat it. Before I put the first spoonful in my mouth, an uncommon commotion outside the train draws our attention away from eating. There is a lot of running, shouting, screaming, several shots and then complete silence. For a long time we sit motionless, looking at each other. What has happened? The fat woman comes back alone, the two pots and the kettle she carries are empty.

She is crying loudly and the layers of fat around her enormous waist shake uncontrollably. In sobs she relates the story. Her companion escaped from the guards and vanished in the thick, tangled undergrowth of the forest. The soldiers pursued him for a while but soon gave up the chase and opened fire. We hope that the bullets fired into the darkness missed him, but this we will never know.

We have been travelling now for over a week. Every day more and more people in our carriage are becoming ill. They are sick and use 'the hole' frequently. The curtain is very dirty and torn in many places. The stench is nauseating. The tiny windows don't let enough air in and the mild weather encourges flies. Mother has a bottle of cologne in her magic bag and several times a day we wipe out hands in a flannel soaked in it. The young baby looks ill. His continuous whimpering is very distressing. His little bottom is sore and the thin short legs are covered with red blotches. To keep the baby dry presents a great problem. Sheets torn into squares, and bits of old towels collected from the people in the carriage, supplement a small bundle of nappies which the baby already has. However, there is nowhere to wash them. The drinking water we get is just enough to keep us going. Therefore, unwashed nappies flutter in the wind, tied to the bars of the windows. As the days go by, they become coarser and coarser and almost orange in colour. I am very worried about the old man on the bench opposite us. He is so weak that he can hardly crawl to 'the hole'. His poor wife squats by his side supporting him.

Chapter 7

News of what goes on in the other carriages is spread by people who are allowed to go out to fetch the boiling water, and it is never good, sometimes almost unbelievable. Ala and I just heard something we were not supposed to hear. Mother and the other women are talking in a muffled fearful whisper. Their shocked faces form ghostly white patches against the darkness of the carriage; three young children died somewhere along the line on this train of unspeakable misery. Their small bodies were pushed through the bars of the windows and thrown off the speeding train. The mothers were not allowed to bury them. Ala and I are lying snuggled closely together. Big, bitter tears stream down our faces, our bodies shake with uncontrollable sobbing. I cover my ears with my hands. I can't bear it! Oh, how I wish I hadn't heard that! Our baby's cry is getting weaker and weaker. I ask God to let the baby live. Next morning mother is worried about us; we look pale and drawn, our eyes are red from crying.

Two weeks have gone by and our journey has not ended yet. We ask the soldiers where we are going, but they either don't know or are not allowed to say. The train has changed direction several times. At one point we thought that we were going northeast towards Siberia. Now after a lot of manoeuvering the train is heading south. We by-pass all the big cities, always at night. We have noticed that this huge undertaking to deport hundred of thousands of Poles to the Soviet Union is conducted in utmost secrecy. Apart from soldiers we never see anyone else at the stopping stations.

We hear sad news again. A couple of teenage boys tried to escape while out to get the water. They were caught almost immediately. They are being held at the stop where they were caught, and will be put on the next train. Their mothers are hysterical. They begged the soldiers to let the boys return to our train but, needless to say, their wishes were not granted. Ala's dramatic reaction to the news surprises mother. Only when it becomes known that the boys who tried to escape were from the carriage next to ours is Ala's calmness restored. "Out of the frying pan into the fire", I say loudly, looking at Ala, hoping that any notion of escape is well out of her mind. In our carriage one lonely young woman is acting very strangely. For hours she stares at the roof of the carriage with glassy eyes. She doesn't talk to anyone and refuses to eat. Mother says that she is very depressed. Her young, new husband was killed in the first week of the war.

Although it is still light, the train has stopped at a small deserted station. I peep through my window to find the reason for this unusual happening. I see a young, crying woman being led out from one of the carriages into an awaiting lorry. With horror I see that our train is departing. Why has she been taken away?! What has she done? We later learn that the woman was about to give birth to a baby. The soldiers decided that she should be taken to the nearest military hospital. She left behind three small children and an old invalid mother. I wonder what will happen to this family and if they will ever be able to find each other in this vast and cruel country.

We are in Central Asia now. "How much longer?" we ask each other. Our legs are stiff from lack of exercise, our backs ache. I know the exact position of each piece of jewellery hidden in the quilt. Mother's bracelet is under my left leg, the thick bulky chain under my right ribs. Ala moans that she can feel rings under her big toe. I suggest that we should swap places but my clever sister generously says that she will suffer all the way.

We don't know what awaits us at the end of our journey, yet we long to get out from the smelly, stuffy, dark carriage. The train speeds onwards in a south-easterly direction. The landscape is changing. Somewhere far on the horizon, enveloped in a foggy mist, the mountains are disappearing from sight. The train changes tracks and after a few hours we stop in the middle of nowhere. It is the end of the line for us. We have been travelling for seventeen days and it is the 1st of May. The rolling, treeless grasslands of Kazakhstan stretch on both sides of the tracks. Several army lorries await us, offensively disturbing the wild, coarse beauty of the endless steppes. The big heavy carriage doors are opened and we all spill out onto the dusty road. What a pathetic, sickly-looking crowd we are! Some people are very ill and have to be carried out, some lean heavily on those who are stronger. The old man is dying, his wife cradles him in her trembling arms, her tired face is blank. Mother tries to console her. She looks at mother with dry eyes and says smiling: "At last he will be in peace and I hope to join him soon". Thank God, mother, Ala and I are well, but we are desperately tired. The rush of fresh air makes us dizzy, the bright sunlight hurts our eyes, and the vast lavish space is overpowering. Once out of the train we all flop on top of our bags and boxes. "What next?" we wonder.

Chapter 8

During our long journey, the soldiers guarding the train have changed several times. Now we see Mongol faces; large, round and flat with slanting eyes and flat, wide noses. They seem to be a little disorientated and not quite prepared for this assignment. Their Russian language is very poor, in fact quite difficult to understand. Once they organise themselves, they start to organise us. There is no rush, no rifles pointing at us. We are too weak to try to escape. Where would we go? Slowly we board the lorries and they start moving off in various directions. We are relieved to see some people we know from Lvov on our lorry. However, mother's friend, John and Mark and other people who occupied the front carriages are going on a little further. The lorry drives in a cloud of dust through roadless steppes. After several kilometres we reach a tiny village; just about a dozen small, very low mud huts. This is Burlaghaz, a miniature Kazakh Kolhoz in the province of Semipalatinsk. A spot surrounded by green-flecked flatness, no trees. Herds of cattle form dark patches on otherwise yellow-green plains. The high, brilliantly white sky is cloudless. A group of curious children and Kazakh officials are waiting for us. One of them, the chief of this Kolhoz (collective farm) informs us that from now on we will live and work among the natives and, in return for our work, we will get some food. We must try not to escape and we must obey the rules of this small community. We are divided into groups and shown the hut in which we are to live.

Our ramshackle mud hut, like the rest of them, is very low and crooked and is still occupied by a herd of goats. As we are not very eager to share our home with goats, we wait outside. Soon a young Kazakh boy leads the animals out of the stable and with a childish smile invites us in. The hut smells and is very dirty. Two square holes in the walls let light in. The wooden door can only be partially closed. There are twelve of us for this one small room. Before we put our luggage on the ground, we get rid of all the goat droppings. While I go to get some water from a well, Ala makes a broom from dry, bushy branches which are scattered outside the hut. We sprinkle some water on the ground to smother the dust and sweep the whole hut thoroughly. We are allowed to get some dry grass which we spread on the ground from wall to wall, to make one long bed. The hay is covered with blankets and quilts. The opposite side of the room is filled with our belongings. As the weather is very warm we have a couple of spare blankets which are fixed to the wall to cover its dirty and rough surface.

I am content, the place looks quite cosy. What I don't see are the thousands of cockroaches, beetles, centipedes and fleas hiding in the hay and in the dark corners, ready to pounce. Unaware of their presence, we stretch our aching bones on the makeshift, communal bed. I look up at the ceiling and scream with horror. The whole ceiling is covered with cockroaches and beetles and they are poised to drop on top of us. "We are not going to stay in this place!" we shout, trembling. Mother tries to calm us down. "They don't do any harm. We will just have to get used to them", mother says, but I can see that she too is very upset. The light-coloured blankets are already taken over by fleas. The whole place is alive with insects.

The first night is a nightmare. Mother stays awake all night picking up the cockroaches and bugs from our tired, curled-up bodies.

Next day we try to smoke them out by making torches from hay, but it doesn't help, they soon come back. The only way to get rid of them is to burn the whole village, and this is exactly how we feel! Although we are covered in flea bites, we are slowly getting used to all the insects, but a constant war is going on and they are winning every time. The worst are the lice, and we get them from Kazakh women and children who visit us regularly. They enter our huts unasked, sit on our beds and stare at us. They seldom talk. They look at our clothes and touch everything. They are amazed to see mother's cigarette lighter and her wrist watch, and they admire the pretty tea cups and shiny pots.

The day mother found the first louse in my long hair filled me with revulsion and shame. Ala is horrified and refuses to sleep next to me or even touch me. She announces that I have to have my long thick plaits cut off at once. "Why me?" I cry and cry and cry. Mother cuddles and kisses me and is very cross with Ala. "Don't be silly, soon we are all going to have lice. The natives are covered in them, their sheepskin furs are their breeding place!" mother says, promising me faithfully not to cut my hair. The very worst thing about lice is the fact that they transmit typhus, a dreaded, often fatal, disease. As predicted, very soon we all have lice in our hair, our clothing and they crawl all over our beds. Every seam of our underwear and dresses is lined by fat, juicy lice. Their favourite places are the seams in the armpits of clothing and the waistbands. They settle neatly along the seams forming greyish-white lines. Every morning, as soon as it gets light, before mother goes to work, a battle with the lice begins. She spreads a white piece of sheet around us and for hours combs our hair with a fine comb. As soon as she sees one fall on the sheet, she kills it. And they keep falling and falling. This is an endless task and she has only limited time to do it in before she goes to work. Nits are a real problem. They are tiny and are firmly attached around each single hair. With her broken fingernails she pulls them off, one by one, methodically, patiently. My head presents more problems, as my hair is long and fair and the nits are not easily visible. Ala still insists that my hair should be cut off. But mother knows how unhappy it would make me. She gets some paraffin and once a week rubs it into my head, then for hours my hair is covered with an old towel. Next morning the lice are dead. However, the nits live on; they are indestructible. The paraffin fumes sting my eyes and burn my skin. I suffer in silence; I want to keep my plaits. We wash our clothes in a small brook not far from the village. We use very little soap, because the stock of a few bars of soap which we took with us from Poland is rapidly depleting. But the lice are still there, they don't mind being washed. For the entire two long years we spend in Russia we never got rid of them.

The day after our arrival all the adults go to work. Only the very old and the very ill are allowed to stay in the village. The workers dig trenches, weed sunflower fields or mind the cattle. The weather is getting hotter and hotter. Hot, strong winds blow through endless steppes. Occasionally one can see pillars of sand, twenty metres high, raised by desert whirlwinds. Often I get a weird feeling that I am in hell and the devil is dancing around me. Every time mother comes home from work, she looks more suntanned and more tired. Fine, yellow dust covers her dark hair and heavy eyelids. Her once smooth, soft skin is becoming dry and wrinkled. Her hands are rough and cracked. For her work mother gets a small quantity of cow's milk and some brown flour.

While mother is at work, Ala and I gather dried cowpats from the surrounding steppes. This is our fuel. We wander around the steppes for hours. We collect the cowpats into a large, old sheet and then carry them home. I have become quite an expert and often argue with Ala, because she picks up pats which are too thin or not dry enough. I look for thick and completely dry pats which burn much better and longer. We come home exhausted. The heat is unbearable.

One woman in our hut has a thermometer; it is 40°C in the shade and 57°C in the sun! Late in the afternoon, when it cools down a little, Ala cooks outside on two stones. She makes soup from water and milk with small brown noodles made by her. If she has some spare flour, she bakes a flat pancake, which is our bread. Most of the time we are hungry and yearn for fresh fruit and vegetables. The visions of green orchards and tree branches heavy with ripe, juicy fruit are so real that I am tempted to stretch my arm and pick one.

As the weeks go by the payment for hard labour is getting scarcer. The milk is more watery and the flour coarser. Everyone is beginning to exchange their articles – which are useless in this primitive rough life – for food. Mother exchanged her silk blouse for some hard, yellow cheese, arul, whose origin can be the milk of a camel, cow, goat or sheep. Another dairy product which we can get in limited quantity from the Kazakh women is ajran. It is like yoghourt and is made from sheep's or goat's milk. One native woman in particular makes it better than the others; hers is thick and creamy. Since we don't have any flour left, Ala and I decide to have some of her ajran for supper. We take mother's embroidered scarf for exchange. The woman is not in so we sit on her doorstep waiting for her. We don't have to wait long. In a few minutes she comes back with a couple of goats in front of her. As soon as she sees us, she starts to make a terrible fuss. She shouts, waving her long stick at us. She looks very angry. We run away without the ajran wondering what we have done. We later learn that sitting on someone's doorstep brings bad luck. We never went back for her wonderful ajran.

Chapter 9

Today we made a good transaction. For our black leather suitcase we received one kilo of flour, a large bowl of ajran and some cheese. I am delighted as Ala will be able to make as many pancakes as we like. But Ala, who is always complaining that while baking smoke from the fire stings her eyes, tells me that from now on we are going to take it in turns and I will have to do my share of the cooking. I don't mind, as long as I have something to cook with. I am burning with curiosity to find our how our suitcase is being used. The next day I call on the woman who bought it. In the deep, bottom part of the suitcase, a small baby sleeps; an excellent idea. But the top part, which was much softer and more pliable, is cut into several long, even strips. The woman doesn't speak any Russian, and I don't understand a word she is saying. However, after a week, the woman visits us proudly showing us a bag she had made from the strips of leather. She had plaited the strips together and cleverly joined them into a bag very much like the one mother has.

It is not long before we begin to run out of articles to exchange, and the Kazakhs are running out of food. Their plight is as sorrowful as ours. The only thing which keeps us going is an elusive hope. After work at night we sit under the starry sky, snuggled closely to mother, listening to the women talking; the stories always full of hope. I learn that there are more than one million Poles scattered over Kazakhstan, Uzbekistan, Siberia and in the prisoner of war camps. Soon, very soon, we will be released and be back in Poland. "It is all a terrible misunderstanding. Someone, somewhere remembers us. The American and English Red Cross are bound to do something." Mother mentions an influential friend who holds an important position in the Italian government; someone else has a rich uncle in Brazil.

We hope that this magical release will come before the merciless winter. "It is only a matter of time", we keep repeating. But already time is running out for some of us. People are dying from dysentery. Poles as well as natives. The illness is short and sharp. Natives die within two to three days, Poles hang on a little longer. No medicines, no hygiene; the illness prevails. Toilets of course are non-existent. The surrounding steppes, with small, dry bushes sparsely scattered over them, provide a retreat for some privacy. Swarms of big, green horseflies buzz constantly and it is hot, very, very hot. In a neighbouring village several people died in one day. Mother is desperate. The water and milk have to be boiled for a long time before we can drink it. Every bit of food is thoroughly covered against the stubborn flies and we constantly wash our hands.

Today a young Kazakh woman died in the hut next to ours. As soon as she died, a few women came and they wrapped her body in a white sheet. They sat around her and cried and laughed alternately, and drank tea. This ceremony repeated itself three times. Afterwards a part of the roof of the hut was removed to allow for the woman's spirit to fly away. Then she was put on a two-wheeled cart pulled by a horse and driven very fast to a burial place. Five elderly men accompanied her. A narrow but very deep grave was dug and she was lowered into it in a sitting position. Before the grave was filled with soil, she was covered with fresh cow's manure.

Mother is not going to work today and this is most unusual. We are very worried that she has caught the dreaded illness. But she assures us that it is only her gall bladder, which used to bother her even before the war. She is sick, has abdominal pain and the whites of her eyes are yellow. Outside the hut the foreman, sitting on his horse, insists that she must go to work. "No work, no food!" he shouts, waving his whip about. He warns her that, if she resists any longer, he will have to take her away from us and put her in prison. His chilling words fill us with fear. Ala volunteers to do mother's work until she gets better. To our surprise and great relief he agrees. Mother and I spend the whole day getting rid of lice from our clothing and hair. I now kill them mercilessly between my fingernails.

Within the first week of our arrival in Burlaghaz, mother

and Ala wrote several letters to friends and relatives in Poland, hoping that a Kazakh to whom they were given will post them one day in a small town Georgiyevka 30 kilometres away. Many weeks have passed since then and we have no replies. We are very worried about father, wondering where he is and whether he is still alive.

Work is getting scarce, so is food. For the past week mother hasn't had to go to work. It is nice to have her around, but what will we eat? "No work, no food", the foreman had said. Mother hopes that the jewellery she has hidden in the quilts will now start to become useful. She doesn't want to exchange her precious mementos of happier times for a mere kilo of flour or a litre of goat's milk. Her wedding anniversary ring or the antique brooch she got from father for Christmas deserve to be valued more highly. Making discreet inquiries she learns that not far from Burlaghaz are gold mines and in a nearby town one can sell gold. She gets her chunky gold chain out from the quilt and together with a couple of friends they set off.

The town is only about ten kilometres away, but the extreme heat and strong wind makes the journey very tiring. Mother's shoes are kept together with a piece of string. Thankfully on the way back they get a lift from a Kazakh driving a cart pulled by oxen. They get home late at night, very tired but happy. We now have sugar, tea, salt, bread, lard, soap and some roubles. Mother warns us not to eat too much at once as our stomachs have been deprived for so long, especially of fat, that she is afraid we may get ill. I look at the lovely creamy-white lump of lard and my mouth waters. Every time mother turns away, I nibble a bit of lard.

Today Ala is not going with me to gather the dry cowpats. She says that she is very busy. She is starting to write a diary in case, in years to come, we forget our miserable experiences. I look at her dumbfounded. Surely, she can't forget. I am sure I could never forget. I point out to her that she shouldn't be wasting paper which is needed to write letters. But Ala is not using the last few pages of our writing pad. She cuts off edges from an old newspaper which she found lying around. She has several long, yellowish strips of paper which are free from print. I admire her ingenuity, but think it is a waste of time.

I like wandering around the steppes with Ala. We always talk and visualize our return to Poland and our meeting with father. We never have any doubts that this will happen very soon. As Ala is not with me today I am lonely and I feel unusually tired. My stomach feels peculiar and I am nauseated. I begin to think that I must have nibbled a little too much of the lard. My bag is only half full of dung but, in spite of this, I sit down on the ground and gaze at the steppes. A group of shaggy camels stroll lethargically towards the village. Tumbleweeds roll across the steppes. A gust of wind lifts some of them up; they twirl in front of my tired eyes and make my head spin.

I am cross with myself. I shouldn't have eaten that lard! I urgently want to go to the toilet. With horror I see blood and mucus, lots of it. I have dysentery. Sweat breaks out all over me. The surrounding steppes seem more hostile than ever. The distance separating me from the village grows larger with each step. I have to stop several times before I reach home. At once mother knows that I am ill. Her anguished face tries to smile: "Don't worry, I will make you better", she says. She gets out a piece of jewellery from the quilt and begs one of the Kazakhs to take her on his cart to 'the gold town'. Ala is to look after me. After several hours she comes back with the rice and dried bilberries. She cooks the rice for a long time until it disintegrates and becomes like a thick, white paste. She feeds me with it slowly, spoonful after spoonful. It tastes horrible but I eat it because I very much want to get better. She brews some bilberries and makes a dark aromatic tea which I drink. Several days pass and there is no improvement. I get up countless times to go to the toilet. Buzzing flies follow me. Every time the journey seems longer and longer. Only yesterday a small clump of dry bushes in the direction in which I am heading seemed to be growing not too far away from the hut, but today it is beyond my reach. My feeble legs feel like jelly and can hardly carry me. Mother gets one of our cooking utensils, puts some cold ash from the burned dung on the bottom of it, and this is my pot. She empties it frequently far away in the steppes. Three times a day mother feeds me with the rice paste and bilberry tea. I force it down my throat hoping for a miracle, but I am beginning to fear the worst and am truly thankful that the corpses of Poles don't get covered in cow's manure during the burial ceremony. On the tenth day mother's tired red eyes are smiling. "Barbara, today I only had to empty your pot twice; you are on your way to recovery!" she says.

Chapter 10

Though it is still dawn, the hut is already hot and stuffy inside. We wake up slowly. Buzzing flies and the multitude of other insects have been awake for hours. Another dawn, another day. Suddenly we hear a loud Kazakh voice and a long horse whip appears through the hole in the wall. "Get up! Get up! there is work for some of you!" he shouts. We crawl out of our beds in a stupor. There is work for five people only. Some are told to go the fields several kilometres away, some are to clean the farm's tractors. Mother is told to mind a large herd of bulls, far away in the steppes. She pales and starts to tremble and with determination, which I have never seen in her before, she refuses. She says that she is ready to do any job, no matter how hard it is, but she is not going to mind the bulls. She would rather go to prison. She looks fierce and very stubborn. As her Russian language is very good, she can express herself forcibly. We listen to the quarrel in amazement. The Kazakh gives up and rides away. All day we sit inside the hut afraid to go out. What is going to happen now, we wonder. From this memorable day on, mother is not offered another job. The vindictive foreman turns a deaf ear to her plea for work, so consequently no work, no food. The jewellery and the gold coins are rapidly depleting. I am unable to think beyond the time when the last piece of gold will be sold. Mother's fear of bulls and cows is the result of a very terrifying experience when, as a girl of seven, she was taken for a 'ride' on a bull's horns. Afterwards she was very shaken and ill for a long time. I can clearly remember some of our holidays in the countryside. Mother always made sure she was as far away as possible from bulls or cows. Sometimes our walks were very tiring as we used to divert from our path to avoid the peacefully grazing cattle.

We have now been in Burlaghaz for almost four months; it seems more like four years. Every couple of weeks the K.B.G. officials come to the village and every time the head of each family is called to the office. They always ask the same question: your name, age, address in Poland, who we write to, and do we have any news about father. Today mother was told by one of the K.G.B. men that we will be moved to another Kolhoz. Some people say that this is the punishment for mother's refusal to mind the bulls. I think it is good news, as I can't envisage worse living conditions; the approaching severe winter in these huts is unimaginable. And maybe, just maybe, in the new Kolhoz no one will know about mother's crime and she will be allowed to work.

We are to move with two other Polish families to the Russian Kolhoz Razin, thirty kilometres away. Rumours are spread that we will be made to walk it, while our luggage will go by cart. Thankfully the rumours are not true. We only walk part of the way. In the next village a cart pulled by oxen is waiting for us. Razin is much bigger than the unforgettable Burlaghaz. There is one small shop and a post office. The most pleasing sight is the trees. There are not many of them but their cool shade is very welcome. Vast potato fields on the outskirts of the village give hope for some work.

We are sharing a small house with a Russian family. Five young children and their mother; the father is in the Red Army. Our sleeping place is a small alcove adjoining a big, hot stove. At night we are practically baking as the weather is still very warm. The nights are always disturbed by the children's crying. Some nights all five of them cry together. We thought that there were a lot of lice in Burlaghaz! This place is unbelievable! The blankets are in motion because of them. My hair, more so than Ala's, is full of the nasty creatures! The woman doesn't mind sharing her home and her lice with us. Often we join in the family's meal, which consists of watery cabbage soup and home-made brown bread. After a few weeks we decide to move out. The lice and the sleepless nights are unbearable. Our sleeping place is more like a torture chamber. With money that we have from selling one of the last pieces of jewellery, together with another family, we rent a small dilapidated house on the outskirts of the village. The house consists of one fairly large room with a stove in it. A small barn attached to the front of this dwelling is in a derelict state. A few hay stacks and some rusty bits from an old plough occupy one part of it. There are no windows in the barn, but several holes in the roof let light in. Ala and I are very pleased. This is like a palace. Only six of us for such a large room! There is no furniture. We make beds from large grey bricks which are themselves made from a mixture of mud, straw and cows' manure. We arrange bunches of dry small bushes and straw on top and cover them with blankets. We sweep the threshing floor and block several holes in the window panes. We share this house with a young Polish woman whom we call auntie, her nine-month-old son Jan and an elderly woman whom we call granny. The fleas and the cockroaches are already there. The lice are transported by us; we are their hosts.

In Razin mother is allowed to work. Ala, who is over fifteen now, in spite of mother's protests is made to go to work also. Together they leave for work very early in the morning and have to walk a long way. They thresh grain, clean the machines, weed the fields or dig potatoes. Payment is very poor. The flour which we get now is full of opium from the masses of poppies which grow in the corn fields. It is so terribly bitter that I refuse to eat it. I look at the watery soup with the brown, horribly bitter noodles floating in it and I can't force myself to have any. Mother and Ala are getting very cross with me. Ala shouts that I will die from starvation. I probably will, I think to myself. Whenever they work in the potato fields, they come home with a few small potatoes cleverly concealed in their clothing. Mother saves them for me. I have noticed that Ala begins to dislike me. "You are a horrid, spoiled brat", she often says. Sometimes we get a piece of home-made bread from a Russian woman who lives next door. Mother seldom has any; the piece is usually divided evenly between Ala and me. I nibble at the piece slowly, savouring its delicious taste.

It is autumn now, and suddenly the weather is getting much colder. With the first frost we get the very first letters from Poland. Ala gets a letter from a best friend in Lvov. Her friend describes her hard life in occupied Poland. Ala reads it aloud and her eyes are full of tears. "She should be here to know what hard life means", I comment. The second letter is from a friend of mother's. We learn from the letter that one of our uncles has been killed and his wife, who is mother's sister, is ill. A food parcel and some money are on their way to us. We pray to God that they will reach us before winter and won't get lost en route. We plan to buy some winter clothes, especially high winter boots, which are made from one piece of hard thick, dark grey felt. They look very clumsy but are light and roomy. One can put a lot of rags inside to keep one's feet warm. Yearningly we wait for the parcels. Out of three parcels which were sent to us, we receive two plus some money. We share it with the three people who live with us. Little Jan needs some more nourishment. Lately he has been crying a lot and he looks very pale. The Russian friend who occasionally gives us some bread, gets sugar and tea; in return she gives us some eggs. We also get a parcel from mother's brother. We buy one large pair of felt boots and for a while our stomachs are full. But the prospects are very bad. People are dying from starvation, typhus and dysentery. Ala has a friend who lives in the village next to ours. Very recently three members of her family died from starvation. We are very upset and worried.

It is only October but the temperature is already 20°C below zero. The locals tell us that this is just the beginning, much worse is still to come. Ala is very prone to colds and tonsillitis. Now her throat is so swollen that she can hardly talk. Mother puts hot poultices around her neck and paints her throat with iodine. Today, apart from a cold, she has a very nasty toothache. One Russian woman, who comes to visit us, consoles her: "Don't worry, a dentist is due to come to this village in two months time, it won't be long now". Although I know it is not a laughing matter, I can't stop laughing. Even Ala sees the funny side of it. Ala's tooth gets better on its own. A visiting dentist doesn't treat teeth, he just pulls them out without any anaesthetic. Ala really is lucky not to have had his attention.

Chapter 11

Every day Ala or I run to the post office hoping for letters or parcels. The day we get our first news from father is a day of renewed hope. Mother sheds quiet tears of joy. We read and re-read the neatly written card and kiss it several times. The cold and gloomy room suddenly becomes warm and cosy. I promise myself faithfully to eat the bitter noodles; I have to get a little plumper before father sees me.

The message on the card is very short. Father is well and hopes we are bravely overcoming all the difficulties. He asks for a photograph of the three of us. The card was written five months ago and it was first sent to Lvov to my parent's friends, whose fate is the same as ours; they are somewhere in Kazakhstan. By some miracle it was handed to a man who knew our whereabouts and he forwarded it to us. The card bears a Moscow post office stamp and it has been censored. We write back to father immediately. We too are very well and everything is just fine. Father is allowed to write one letter a month. The letters come first from Starobelsk, then Kozelsk and Gryazovets. He doesn't write much but we are satisfied; he is alive. In one letter he sends us a pencil-drawn sketch of himself, drawn by one of his fellow prisoners. He doesn't look like the father we remember. His face is lined and thin and he looks very sad. He adds in the letter that his pocket mirror tells him that he looks better.

Winter is here; it is getting very cold. The very first strong snowstorm of the winter strengthens our sense of vulnerability in this little old house. A blustering wind is raging outside. Thank goodness it is Sunday and mother and granny don't have to go out in this weather. Ala is in bed again with a severe attack of tonsillitis. The wind howls in the chimney, blowing soot and grit into the room. Cracked window panes rattle. The thick layers of old newspapers, which only a few minutes ago were covering the numerous holes in the panes, are now fluttering in the air letting snow in. A second window which is just above the bed on which Ala is lying with a high fever and swollen throat, squeaks ominously. A big crack appears between the window frame and the wall and the frame starts to wobble to and fro. Suddenly one small section of the wall caves in and about half a dozen crumbling, grey bricks tumble down on top of Ala, followed by drifting snow and gusts of icy wind. Mother rushes towards Ala but, seeing that apart from a small superficial graze on her arm she is fine, grabs a blanket and, with granny's help, quickly blocks the big hole with it. The wind is so strong that they have to hold it with their bodies spread-eagled across it. "Get some help, but don't go any farther than the next house!" mothers warns me. I jump into our huge felt boots, wrap my head in a large woollen scarf and run out of the house. As the wind is against me, it takes me all my strength to battle my way across the snow-covered road. Thankfully our neighbour's husband is in. From his barn he collects a few thick wooden boards and some tools and, without a word, follows me back to our house. Very skilfully he boards up the hole and, to make certain that the rest of the shaky wall is more stable, he safeguards it by nailing several planks of wood here and there. Following his advice we move our communal bed to the opposite side of the room, hoping the wall will hold and see us through the winter.

Strong blizzards are everyday occurrences. Some days the snow storms are so fierce that no one leaves the house. Roads disappear beneath thick blankets of snow. We try to keep our stove alight by burning branches and cowpats. It is a very tedious chore as the once dry branches and dung which we collected and stored in the barn for the winter are now very damp. It takes two hours to boil the kettle. Often the strong wind blows the black smoke back into the room. We quickly smother it, but the smoke chokes us and burns our eyes. Jan cries and cries but the windows are blocked by snow drifts and we can't open them. Our toilet, a small shed at the back of the house, has ceased to exist. It is completely buried under the snow. For a few weeks now we have been using the barn as our toilet. The barn is already partially filled by snow which drifts through the holes in the roof. Thanks to the severe frost, hygiene as yet is not a problem. This unavoidable arrangement worries me. I don't dare to think of spring, when several layers of human waste will start to thaw.

Mother now works nights as a night-watchman. She guards several sheep which are kept in a large enclosure outside the village. Dark, bitterly cold nights are spent walking around the enclosure, sounding a gong and blowing a whistle to frighten the wolves away. Some nights the wolves sneak very near and when she can see their yellow eyes glistening in the darkness she gets very scared. She has to be vigilant because if, by any chance, a wolf gets its prey the night-watchman doesn't get paid for a long time to compensate for the loss of a sheep. Granny also works at night. She looks after ninety pigs and cleans their sties. She brings home the most ghastly stuff with which the pigs are fed. It is some kind of food tightly pressed into big, grey lumps; her pockets are full of it. Although I promised myself to eat the bitter noodles, I never promised to eat this revolting stuff. I cry and pretend that I am sick and not at all hungry. Mother gives in and asks the good neighbour for some more bread. As soon as we get a parcel, she repays her handsomely. But the parcels are few and far between.

One night I had a very enjoyable dream. I am sure it means prosperity. I dreamt that I was dressed in a lovely, long gown with a train. The gown was made from thick slices of streaky bacon. Pink and white strips were arranged in a very pretty pattern. I was coming down wide marble steps in some magnificent house. With every step I took, the greasy, long train rubbed against the marble, making it shine. Ala was sitting at the bottom of the stairs; she was dressed in green and looked like a cabbage. When I told Ala about my dream she said that the only thing it meant was that I was a very greedy girl who only thought of food. I will never share my dreams with her again.

Ala now works indoors, cleaning the warehouses. One day she comes home after work, feeling very ill. She is nauseated and has a severe headache. We think she has been poisoned by the fumes from the chemicals which she uses to wash down the walls. I am told to go to our neighbour and ask for one egg and some milk. Mother whisks the white of the egg and mixes it with milk. Ala drinks it and after a short while she feels better, but she stays in bed a couple of days. While in bed, she writes her diary regularly and very secretly. Now she uses proper paper which she can sometimes get in the little shop. The long strips of newspaper edges which she used in Burlaghaz proved not very satisfactory; the letters are smudged and very unclear. "In forty years time I won't be able to read it at all", she says. How can anyone think so far ahead! My vision of the future is meeting with father in our home in Lvov, and this I strongly believe is only a few months away, as soon as this terrible winter finishes.

Though I know that Gogo is dead, I always see father sitting together with Gogo, in a big, leather armchair in our study. A little side table is laid with mouth-watering cakes and Gogo is using all his doggy charm to get one. "What are you thinking about? You are miles away", Ala suddenly says, bringing me back to reality. Oh yes, we are in Razin! Ala is not well and she is writing her diary. I wonder whether in her diary she ever mentions John. Twice John was able to visit us in Burlaghaz and on those two occasions he looked tired and downhearted. I observed them closely and came to the conclusion that Ala was not so keen on John anymore. She remarked that he was too skinny and his hair was very badly cut.

It is getting dark. How can Ala see? Father always told us not to read or write in semi-darkness. "It is bad for your eyes", he used to say. We have no paraffin lamps or candles. Our lighting is very primitive and I am not sure who thought of this invention. A piece of string about five inches long is put through a hole in the centre of a thick slice of raw potato. This is placed on a small plate with some castor oil or paraffin in it. The piece of string gets saturated with the oil and acts as a wick. This device gives very poor light and the smell is nauseating. The days are very short now; it is still dark at 10.00 a.m. But we use our 'potato lamp' only for a short while. There is a shortage of castor oil and paraffin. The delivery to the shops of the important goods is very erratic. Sometimes there is no salt, matches, paraffin or paper for several weeks.

It is Christmas tomorrow and a parcel we were hoping for has just arrived. We now have sugar, tea, rice, semolina, cocoa and some soap. Mother cuts in half one bar of soap and puts a cupful of sugar into a little bag – she then sends me with this small parcel to our Russian neighbour. This is our Christmas present for her. She in return gives us a large piece of freshly-baked bread. Ala and I make a Christmas tree from dry branches of bushes and decorate it with long, thin strips of coloured paper. "It looks like a witch's broom!" I comment. But Ala says I have no imagination. Mother makes beetroot soup and delicious pudding from the rice, sugar and cocoa. Four eggs were also needed, which came from an exchange of food with our neighbour. The scene is set: the 'potato lamp' is burning and the beetroot soup is steaming on the hot stove. We stand around our improvised Christmas tree wishing each other a better and brighter future. There are no presents, but this doesn't worry us. The best and most valuable gift is health, and at the moment we are all well. Although Ala says I have no imagination, she doesn't know how often in my thoughts I am transferred far, far away from here. But today is Christmas Eve and my thoughts are unflinching. I am staying firmly in this cold, dark room with mother, Ala, Jan, his mother and granny, because today of all days I don't want to cry.

Father's card with his Christmas wishes comes six weeks later.

Chapter 12

It is the beginning of 1941 and the fury of winter is at its peak. The temperature is 45°C below zero. The blizzards are very strong and the snow in many places is over five metres high. Our house is almost covered by snow.

We are beginning to understand why this house has stood empty for so many years and is in such a derelict state. It was built on a lower level than the rest of the village and seems to be in a ditch. As a result of its unfortunate position it is uninhabitable during the winter. It is permanently dark inside the house as the snow is well above the windows. Every time we want to leave the house we have to dig our way out, a very tiring task. We are seriously worried that soon we will be completely buried under the snow. This happens the day mother is trying to start the fire under the stove, as she does every morning; but the pieces of wood and dung, instead of catching alight, start smoking. Curling clouds of dark smoke gush back into the room. We realise at once that our chimney is blocked by snow. We try to open the front door but the undertaking is hopeless. Several tons of snow are obstructing the exit. We smother the choking smoke and look at each other with horror. What is going to happen now? I imagine that this is our communal grave and we will never get out of here alive. We pray that soon our neighbour will see our plight and someone will dig us out. The anxiety makes us thirsty; we eat the snow, which by now is a metre high in the barn. To give Jan a drink, his mother melts some snow over the 'potato lamp'. Hours are ticking away slowly. The whole day has passed and nothing has happened. Although we can't make a fire it is not very cold inside. The thick blanket of snow envelopes the house keeping the wind off. It is getting very stuffy inside the room, smoke lingers around. We feel tired and lethargic, and go to bed with our clothes on. No one talks, even Jan stops crying. It seems as if time is standing still; it is so very quiet and eerie. How long can we last in a little house buried under the snow? I can't sleep. Cheerless, grim thoughts cram my mind. I stare up at the ceiling but instead of the cracked dirty plaster I see a skating rink and myself on it in a red hat and gloves. Back in Lvov we had a big garden and a tennis court. During the winter the court was transformed into an ice rink on which Ala, a friend and I used to spend many happy hours; we were all quite good skaters. One day my friend and I were enjoying ourselves immensely and decided to ignore my mother's voice calling us back home. I asked my friend to bury me in the snow to hide me from mother's sight before she came looking for us. As I expected, mother appeared shortly and at once saw a heap of snow under which I was hiding. She was very cross with me. "You are a very silly girl, you could have suffocated under this snow, it doesn't take long!" she said. "And now you will probably get a cold; your coat is wet!" she added crossly.

I never asked mother how long it would take to suffocate and I don't think I will ask now. But she was right about the cold. I not only got a cold but pneumonia and I was ill for a long time.

A whole day and night has passed. Nothing is happening. "Why is no one helping us?" We feel helpless and very hungry. We eat more snow. Some rice and flour which we have needs to be cooked but we daren't start a fire. Ala is writing her diary by the tiny flame of the 'potato lamp'. Mother tells her to put the light out as it uses oxygen and the smell is sickening. It is dark again. I feel drowsy. I close my eyes and see father on a big white horse holding a huge shining shovel. He gets off the horse and, with a few quick strokes of the shovel, moves all the snow away from the house. My dream ends suddenly with the unexpected, odd knocks and noises which are coming from the chimney breast. Mother moves hastily towards it, and stretching her hands like a blind person, feels inside the chimney. A small sack tied to a long string descends down into the room. In the sack is a small bottle of milk for Jan, a large bottle of hot water, some bread and a note. Granny lights the 'potato lamp' and reads the note which says that Kolhoz officials have been notified and several men are coming to dig us out. "Keep hope alive, never say die!" Ala says smiling, and making use of the light, quickly writes the words in her diary. Jan's mother starts crying, she kisses and cuddles him and tears of great relief stream down her pale face. Granny is praying aloud.

We wait expecting to hear at any moment the sound of activity through the uncovered chimney. But the absolute silence is very disconcerting. The delay worries us, the anxiety returns. We begin to lose heart, fearing that perhaps the very severe weather prevents the men from rescuing us. Help comes after six long hours. It takes several men another four hours to dig an almost vertical narrow tunnel, like a chimney, to reach our front door which, because of the pressure of the snow, they can only partially open. The bitterly cold, but fresh air reaching us from outside is very welcome; we drink it like a fine wine. The men make a few small steps in the wall of the slippery tunnel to make it easier for us to climb out. From this day they keep an eye on our little house in the ditch, and whenever the blizzards are strong and the snowfall is heavy, they come and dig us out. They also remove all the snow from every side of the house, making a corridor several feet high around it. We don't dare think about the big thaw; we will worry about that when the time comes. Our neighbour told us later that the day we were buried alive she didn't come out of her house at all, because the blizzards were far too strong. However, when she ventured out the next day in the afternoon, she was horrified to see what had happened. She uncovered our chimney with the help of her husband to give us some food and raised the alarm.

The day after our deliverance, I, being the smallest occupant of the house apart from Jan, am sent to the post office. I wrap myself well, put the big felt boots on, and start to scrape my way up the icy tunnel. The task is not easy. I have so many clothes on that I can hardly move, and the bulky boots don't grip the little, slippery steps. Every time I almost reach the top I slide down like a fat sausage in a tilted frying pan. Ala is getting annoyed, saying that I am either making a game out of it, or I am very clumsy. Eventually I am practically thrown out into the open by four pairs of hands which are pushing me up from inside. Once outside I look around agape; I am astounded. Our house and a couple of fairly tall trees growing nearby are non-existent! Mountains of snow heaped into drifts have changed the familiar surroundings into a bewildering, featureless whiteness. The neighbouring houses on the opposite side of the road are half buried in snow, but the crooked roofs and cracked chimneys are visible.

In the post office a parcel and two letters are waiting for me. I put the letters in my pocket and carry the parcel by its string. The blizzard has died down and the day is very calm. Brilliant white snow glistens in the sunlight and is very crisp. As I am very anxious to see what is in the parcel, I decide to shorten my way back home through a field. I only walk a short distance when I suddenly feel that my feet are sinking. I try to pull my legs out of the snow but, every time I do, the big boots hinder my every move and they don't budge. I am sinking deeper and deeper. I let go of the parcel to have two free hands to assist me in my struggle. I am beginning to feel very tired and the snow is almost to my waist now. I panic; the more I scramble the deeper I seem to be sinking. There is no point in shouting, no one will hear me. The houses are too far away and I don't see anyone around. The blizzard is coming back, the wind is getting stronger and it is starting to snow. The parcel which is only a couple of feet away from me in disappearing beneath the falling snow. The panic which I felt only a few minutes ago is gone. I feel warm and blissfully dizzy. The whiteness around me dazzles my eyes. I close my eyelids and feel increasingly more sluggish and weary. I am falling asleep. Suddenly, vigorous jerks wake me from my stupor. Someone is pulling me out of the snow. I see the postman's worried face bent over me. "Another few minutes, little girl, and you would be completely covered by snow", he says. Once out of the snow, it becomes apparent that my big boots are still firmly lodged deep down in it. The postman gets them out and we start looking for the parcel, but we have to abandon our search because by now the mighty blizzard is getting very strong. The postman sees me to my home and I slide down the hole in tears.

As the days go by we make our tunnel wider by hacking at the icy snow with a dull piece of iron found in the barn. Now, apart from granny and Jan, we can all go out, but we have to take it in turns as we only possess one pair of boots suitable for this weather. Ala has not been to work for a couple of weeks; she seems to have a constant cough and sore throat. But mother, weather permitting, tries not to miss her night work. I never thought winter could be so long and so severe. Even the natives, who are used to this extreme cold, are found frozen to death on roads. Frost-bitten ears, fingers and toes are very common. My toes are swollen and dreadfully painful. And, although we never go out without a head cover, both of Ala's ears are inflamed and itching. They look considerably larger, which mortifies her; she fears that they might never shrink back to their original, dainty size.

Chapter 13

At the beginning of March it gets noticeably warmer. I look at the heaps of yellow snow mixed with human waste in our barn and I feel sick. Soon it will start to melt and will trickle into our room. One night in the middle of March, the big thaw starts. The rumbling sound of heavy lumps of snow sliding down the roof wakes us up. Not only can we hear water dripping all around the house, but we can also hear it gushing into the room from the barn. Carefully I pull my arm out from under the cover and touch the ground. Shivers run down my spine as my hand feels the icy water. Our beds are surrounded by it. I am grateful it is pitch dark in the room and I can't see what floats in it. "We are flooding!" granny cries. Everyone gets out of bed in haste, apart from me. I just can't pluck up enough courage to plunge my bare feet into this horrid water. Ala, seeing my hesitation, practically pushes me out of the bed. We retrieve our shoes which by now are completely drenched. Hopefully once they dry they will still be serviceable. We hear water dripping all around us, and see dirty water rushing in from the barn. Every pot, pan and pail is used to scoop out the murky, smelly water. Our bare feet are numbed by cold and the skirts tucked around our waists are getting splashed. Five of us are working very hard all through the night, but the water keeps coming in faster and faster. There is still a lot of snow left in the barn and the huge wall of it surrounding the house has hardly moved. We pile our belongings on top of the beds to save them from the flooding. Little Jan sits on top of them, watching us with interest. He claps his hands and laughs. Oh, how I would love to change places with him! Our granny, the oldest member of this household, impresses me. Her stamina is remarkable. Her dress is wet and her hands, deformed by arthritis, are blue, but she is unflagging. "We can't give up", she says firmly. Large grey bricks with which the beds are made are half covered by water. Soon our quilts, blankets and clothing will be ruined. Mother rushes out to get some help; she is back quickly with two men. They knock out two large holes in the walls, one on each side of the house, to let the water out. For several days we have a continuous stream of water running through our home. I am convinced that the melting snow from the entire village flows through this little house in the ditch. The walls are soaked with water. We are surprised that the house has not collapsed yet, but who knows, it might still do that! I hope we will not be in it when it happens! We promise ourselves that if we have to spend another winter in Russia it won't be in this house.

The dampness in the room is dreadful; our blankets and clothing have a horrible, unhealthy, mouldy smell about them. Somehow we seem to be taking everything in our stride. Apathy is setting in. To start a fire under the stove is a great achievement. Even with the help of several old newspapers the saturated wood takes hours before it catches fire. On some days we can't have our first hot drink until the afternoon. Let's get through one day at a time. The merciless winter is behind us; the big thaw is nearing its end. Now only a small trickle of water runs through our room. Soon it will all dry up and the long, scorching summer will begin. Meantime Ala gets another bad cold; she keeps us awake at night coughing. Granny is bitterly complaining that all her bones are aching; her knees are swollen and inflamed. Jan gets a very itchy rash all over his small body; he scratches his legs and arms till they bleed. We are worried that he caught some awful illness from the filthy water. But thank God the rash disappears after a few days and he gets better. I keep well but am constantly hungry.

One year in exile has passed. Mother and her friends still talk about a miracle release. Only the hope of a better future keeps us going. I don't think of the past any more, what is the point? It will never be the same again. Mother gets very concerned that a whole year has passed and we have not been to school. We don't even have any books to read. Ala decides to teach me mathematics, the subject which I loathe the most and was never any good at. After a couple of sessions and a lot of arguments, Ala gives up saying that I don't concentrate and if I want to grow up not even knowing my tables, it is fine with her. One day granny comes home from work announcing proudly that she has a teacher for us. She met an old friend, a man of seventy, who used to be a professor of astronomy at the University of Lvov. He has just been transferred from another Kolhoz and is now staying in Razin. He is very keen to teach us and is looking forward to the meeting. This news depresses me greatly. Why should I start learning about astronomy if, according to Ala, I don't know my tables? Mother assures us that granny's friend will teach us more down-to-earth subjects. How very wrong she is! The first lesson is full of heavenly bodies; Mars, Venus, Jupiter. I nudge Ala but I think she is enjoying it. The second lesson is even more advanced. During the third lesson we are already calculating the distances between the stars! I can't endure it any longer. I pretend to be ill and leave Ala with the old man. She comes home furious saying that she is not going there any more all by herself.

As soon as the ice and the snow melts, the wind and increasingly warmer weather dries our house and the surroundings very quickly. It is hard to imagine that only a few weeks ago this little village was almost hidden beneath the thick snow and was cut off from the rest of the world. Mother and Ala work in the fields again. They have to walk a long way to reach them, leaving early in the morning and returning home late at night. Ala complains bitterly that her feet are sore, as she is not used to walking barefoot. The shoes which we had are in tatters now. To get some money to buy shoes, mother decides to sell her last piece of jewellery, her beautiful diamond engagement ring. She gets it out of the quilt and for a long time looks at it with misty eyes. "I was only seventeen when father gave it to me", she says. She tries to put it on but it is too tight. "My goodness, the ring doesn't fit me any more, my hands are so swollen and rough now!" she adds quietly. Ala looks at me, I look at Ala. "You can't sell it! You promised to give it to your first granddaughter!" we cry spontaneously. "Today or tomorrow a parcel or money are bound to come, let's hold on a little longer!" We wait. I force myself to eat the horrible, bitter noodles. Ala stops complaining that her feet are sore. She tries to hide from mother the big red blisters on the soles of her feet. After four long weeks we get a parcel and some money from friends. We breathe a sigh of relief; for a while at least the ring is safe. We buy coarse, clumsy sandals in the small town of Georgiyevka; we are happy, they are better than nothing.

For the last few days mother and Ala have had a lift home from work from a Kazakh who drives a cart pulled by an ox and lives in a village close to Razin. This most unexpected comfort gives mother and Ala more time to rest at home. The Kazakh is very friendly and talks a lot in his broken Russian. He gives Ala big pieces of his pancake-like bread which we all share. He comes to our home quite often now and always has a round, flat bread hidden under his dirty sheepskin coat. Sometimes he also has a lump of hard cheese wrapped in a piece of cloth. Mother tries to give him some of our tea or rice in exchange but he always refuses. Why is he so kind to us, I wonder? Soon we begin to know the reason. The reason is Ala. His narrow slanting eyes don't leave Ala's face and he always sits next to her on our communal bed. Every time he does that, Ala moves away. "He smells of goats", she whispers in Polish. I am enjoying the whole situation immensely but Ala and mother don't find it funny. Now, as soon as he comes, Ala leaves the room and mother obstinately refuses his bread. I think that the amorous Kazakh is just as stubborn as mother. Today just before he left us, he placed a few pancakes on our window sill. "We are not going to touch them", mother says looking sternly at me, "Next time he comes he will know he is not welcome." "It is such a terrible waste and I am very hungry!" I say to mother, almost crying, and I begin to wonder whether she would notice if I have one. Next morning, soon after mother, granny and Ala leave for work and auntie is busy dressing Jan, I can't control myself any longer. I snatch one and quickly eat it. It was already getting stale but that didn't spoil my enjoyment. In the evening, without fail, the Kazakh arrives, places some more pancakes on the window sill and walks away. "How long are we going to play this silly game with him?" I ask mother. "As long as it is needed", mother says. "And don't be tempted to eat one like you did today", she adds. On the third day, looking very formal, he places yet another stack of pancakes on the window sill, walks right into the house and openly tells

Surviving snapshots of the time are few and precious but, understandably, not of the best quality.

(i) Above. My sister Ala and I on holiday in Poland, 1938.

(ii) Right. Out of Russia. Father, mother and I at Pahlavi, August 1942.

"Mother's bright red dress with large yellow flowers is hilarious; everytime we look at her we burst out laughing."

(iii) My pet and I, aged 14. Masindi, Uganda. January 1944.

(iv) Postcard of the Polish Camp, Masindi.

(v) The occupants of the hut. Masindi 1944.

(vi) Top left: Ala and I on the Nile. Murchison Falls Expedition. 1946.
(vii) Top right: Father with a young owl. 1946.
(viii) Below: Out of Africa. Ala and I in England. July 1948.

mother that his intentions are honourable and he would like to marry Ala as he is a widower and needs a young wife to look after his two small children. He assures mother that Ala and we will have plenty of bread, cheese and goats milk. His round, moon-like face breaks into a broad, friendly smile, and the dark narrow eyes look searchingly for his bride-to-be. As soon as I hear his generous proposition I run out of the room laughing hysterically. Ala, who is hiding in the outside shed, is furious, saying that I am extremely silly and childish. To annoy her even more I tell her that she should have pretended to like him for the simple reason that the bread he gets out from under his sweaty and louse-infested armpit is much better than the course, bitter flour we have. Because she calls me silly, childish and a lot of other very nasty names, I plan to tell John about their romance once we meet again. As soon as my outburst of laughter subsides, burning with curiosity, I sneak back into the room, but by then the Kazakh and regretfully also all three piles of his pancake-like bread are gone. From this day we never see him again.

Chapter 14

Today we received two cards from father which were sent several weeks ago. Although they were posted a month apart, we got them the same day. The cards are almost identical. Father is well and in both of them he wants to know if we have any opportunity to listen to the radio or read the newspapers. We think that father is trying to tell us that there is something going on in the world of which we are not aware. As far as we know there is no radio in the whole village and whenever we get hold of a newspaper the news is old and very scarce. We hear rumours. The stories are spread by word of mouth and the fact that very recently a lot of young men from the village were drafted into the Red Army proves that the world is in turmoil. We don't know how this will affect us, but we hope and pray to God that we won't be forgotten. Since our neighbour's husband was taken into the army, she comes to us more often and she usually cries. She has four young children and she is expecting the fifth in a couple of months. Whenever she receives a letter from her husband she asks mother to read it to her. She is not the only one. We are amazed to see how many adults in this village can't read or write.

The war between Russia and Germany breaks out in June. A terrible gloom falls over the village. The woman weep openly but they whisper: "Why should we fight for Stalin? He gave us nothing but misery. Our life is hard and is going to be even harder." We hear news that Lvov has been taken by the Germans, that our lovely city is in ruins and the German army is marching east. The K.G.B. men come to Razin, they check and re-check all the Polish families. The letters and the parcels stop arriving from Poland. The last letter Ala has from her friend is very brief and full of apprehension.

Poland, torn between two powerful enemies, is lying low, waiting. Living conditions in Razin are becoming even more unbearable. We hear of people eating the meat of dead camels to stay alive. Owing to the intense summer heat and lack of food, the resistance to disease is minimal. Starvation and disease are our greatest enemies. Night blindness and scurvy are very common. Mother thinks that our neighbour's two youngest children have scurvy, as their mouths are sore and they have swollen and painful joints. Several Poles suffer from night blindness. Our granny has difficulty breathing and she says this is due to the very hot weather. Jan keeps well, yet he doesn't seem to be growing. He is very thin and pale. Some days mother comes home from work so weary that she can hardly stand. The blazing sun is merciless and there is no shade in the open fields. To make matters even worse, the workers have not been paid for a couple of weeks now. The foreman assures everyone that the food will arrive soon. He blames the delay on the war. "The soldiers who are fighting for our country have a priority, they have to be fed before anyone else." Mother sells one of our quilts, making sure first that she has not left a gold coin or a small piece of jewellery inside it. Unfortunately there is nothing left, apart from her engagement ring which she now keeps in a bag. I am a little worried that now we are only left with one quilt. During the winter they were indispensable, but mother says that we can't think about tomorrow as it is today that we have to eat.

Today I overheard a very strange story. Apparently some young Polish woman 'sold herself' to a Russian man for food. I must admit I don't understand the whole meaning of it, but I feel very disturbed. When I asked mother, I noticed her blush. She told me that this woman must have married the man although she didn't love him, to make her life a little easier. "Hunger can drive some people to the most drastic actions", she said. I am not totally satisfied with her answer, and I wonder for a while whether Ala can explain it to me better, but after second thoughts, I don't think I will bother.

I have always been told at home and at school to be good and completely honest, so it is only natural that one thing worries me a little. Yesterday very late at night, an elderly Russian man, whom we knew quite well and who is a storekeeper in Razin's warehouse, brought us about four kilos of flour in exchange for some sugar and soap of which we still have a small amount. He was very secretive about it all and told us many times to hide the flour well. It was obvious that he had stolen it. I share my thoughts with mother and Ala and I am surprised to hear mother say that everything depends on circumstances. Ala reminds me about the potatoes which I ate with great relish although I knew very well that they too were stolen.

Rain in this part of the world comes seldom but, when it does, it is torrential. Recently we had a most spectacular storm. Suddenly and most unexpectedly, thick and very dark clouds gathered over the village. Bright day changed into night. Thunder rolled across the dark sky growling angrily, zigzag lightning flashed non-stop. The rain was so heavy that it looked like a waterfall. We were afraid that our little house in the ditch would be flooded by water, but the storm which came so suddenly died down within an hour. Rain water, which only a few minutes ago had flowed through the village like a river, was raidly drawn in by the dry, scorched soil. The black clouds disappeared, uncovering a bright blue sky and glaring sun.

I think mother must be the only person in this village who has an umbrella and she uses it often, not against rain but to protect herself and Ala from the sun on their way to work. Every time she uses it she has a crowd of gaping children and women following her and when, amused by this interest, she demonstrates how to open and close it, the surprise on their faces is a pleasure to see. "What a pity we only have one umbrella as I am sure they would be excellent items to exchange for food. Next time we come to Kazakhstan I will bring a couple of dozen of them with me", mother jokes.

Almost two months have passed since the start of the war between Russia and Germany. We hear rumours that all Poles, from every corner of this country, those in prison camps and those deported like us, are now free and can go and do whatever they like. Somewhere in the south-west the Polish army is being formed from all the men who only yesterday were a sick starving crowd in rags; but today this crowd is to fight the Germans, alongside the English,

Russians and half of the world. It is hard to believe that one day the Poles are the enemies of Russia, and the next we are supposed to be friends helping them to conquer the German army. Mother says that it is all politics and now there is hope that we will get our country back. Unrest amongst the Poles in Razin is very evident but we have not been told anything officially. We have heard so many rumours and unfounded stories before, so many times our hopes have been raised. I have visions of father driving his car in a cloud of dust through the Kazakhstan steppes, to get us out of this hell. Whenever the K.G.B. men come to Razin, and they come very often now, mother asks them to allow us to move to the nearby small town of Georgiyevka, but they always refuse. The thought of another winter in our little house in the ditch fills us with horror.

At the beginning of September all the Poles are called to Razin's office. The K.G.B. men are handing out large, blue sheets of paper which say that we are free people now, but we must not go to the big cities or towns or the occupied territory. The paper also states that we are free citizens of Poland. So this is it, we are free. Now we can move to Georgiyevka if we can find accommodation, but that is about all. We can't go anywhere else, we have no money to travel. Impatiently we wait for news from father. Long weeks go by; nothing has changed. The house is just as grim and our stomachs are empty. A couple of freed prisoners of war have already reached Razin and are united with their families; they look like shadows of their former selves. I don't want to hear the stories they tell, they upset me too much. In my mind I see father the way he was two years ago. Healthy and strong with sparkles in his blue eyes. Within the first week one of the freed prisoners dies. The long, difficult journey and meeting with his beloved wife and child was too much for his weak heart.

At last the eagerly awaited letter arrives! Father's usually steady and neat handwriting is different this time. The letters are big and uneven as if they were written by a very shaky hand. "I am still in the prison camp Gryazovets but I am a free man now!! I will be sending some money for your travels. The Polish army is forming in the south; we will all be going there. I hope to see you soon." Ala and I have never seen anyone faint, so when mother faints after reading aloud father's short letter, we think that she has suddenly died. The shock is so great that for a long time after her recovery we can't rejoice.

Chapter 15

Our spirits are high. Once we are together everything is going to be fine. We don't know that there is a long and gruelling road ahead of us. We move to Georgiyevka and again we live with mother's friend, John and Mark, who have been there now for a couple of weeks. They too will be travelling south and John is very eager to join the Polish Army. He looks very different now. The time spent in Russia has transformed him from a young childish boy into a man. Ala doesn't notice his awful haircut any more and says he will look wonderful in soldier's uniform. Parting with granny, Jan and his mother mars our joy of seeing father soon. Jan, whose angelic face was like a ray of sunshine during the past dismal months, is now very sad. His small lips are quivering; he knows that we are leaving. I try hard not to cry and start making funny faces, just to see him smile, but this time I don't succeed. Jan, instead of laughing, bursts into tears and so do I. I shudder to think what will happen to them.

In Georgiyevka one of the K.G.B. men, commenting on mother's good command of the Russian language, promises her work in an office, but it is only an empty promise. She and Ala still have to work very hard. Yesterday the most frightful sand storm caught them in the fields. Huge clouds of sand raised by a violent wind changed day into night, blinding them. Their eyes, mouths, ears and noses were full of gritty sand. They tried to hide in a shed that was standing at the side of the field but, before they could reach it, the shed collapsed and within minutes was covered by sand. Soon large hail-stones pelted down with such force that mother and Ala were badly bruised. This morning they are very tired and achey. "I feel as if I was in a battle", Ala says, looking at several small bruises on her arms.

After a couple of weeks the eagerly awaited money from father arrives. All the prisoners of war, as soon as they were released from camps, were given a small amount of roubles to help them on their way to places where the Polish army was being formed. We pack our bags and say goodbye to John, Mark and their mother. They hope to follow us shortly. I try to imagine our meeting with father and I feel a little scared; the visions of him driving the car or sitting in his study with Gogo are completely erased from my mind. I face reality. Soon I will see him the way he is now. We are to go to Orenburg, one of the rallying points, where father's function is to organise the Polish people on their way to Buzuluk, Kuybyshev and farther south to Kirgizia. Our journey is supposed to take six days.

The journey is an indescribable nightmare. The stations and the trains are overflowing with people; a lot of soldiers, a lot of Russian civilians and a lot of Poles. Because of the war the train's schedules are completely disrupted. Nights and days are spent on station platforms, waiting and waiting. The Poles come from all over Russia; from the Siberian taiga, from Arkhangelsk, Kolyma, Uzbekistan, Kazakhstan and many other God-forsaken places. At night, when we settle to sleep on the platforms, there is not a square foot of free floor space; a carpet of human bodies covers it entirely. Some people are very sick and are in the most pathetic state, but they are all going to join the Polish Army. At one station we sit next to a young woman who buried her husband and three children in Siberia. She tells us of her hope of being taken into the Polish Army. "I might meet my brother there. The last I heard of him he was in Kamchatka", she says with a faint smile. She opens her tattered, dirty bag and takes out a photograph of three, blond, smiling boys. "I left them in taiga", she whispers, her breath drained. Her eyes shine and are almost transparent.

When the train eventually arrives, the mass of people rushes towards the open doors. We fight, shout and cry. Everyone wants to get in, but the train has only limited space. Once completely filled with people, the train stands at the station for several hours. It gets unbearably hot and stuffy but no one dares to leave the train in case they will not be able to get back in.

We have now been travelling for five days and are only half way to Orenburg. During that time we had to change trains several times. The stations are in chaos. Drinking water is often unobtainable, as is food. It is almost impossible to know if one is boarding the right train. Only yesterday we boarded a train which was supposed to be going to Orenburg but after two hours we were told that the train was heading in the opposite direction. In our carriage now is a sad group of emaciated, sick-looking children, who are looked after by one young couple. All of them are orphans; their parents are buried in the Kazakhstan steppes. "How very lucky we are!" I say to Ala. Some people, like us, are travelling to prearranged meeting places with fathers, husbands or brothers, who are now freed from the camps, but a lot of them are just going south. The magical words: "The Polish Army" entices everyone.

We arrive in Orenburg five days late. We are hungry, dirty and weary and we are dreadfully worried that father might not still be here. This station, like all the others, is crowded with people. There are a lot of Russian soldiers about. Several trains are packed with the Red Army. They are going to the front to fight the Germans. Their wives, children and mothers stand around crying. Once out of the train, with great difficulty, we find some free floor space and put our bags into a small heap. I am left behind to mind the luggage while mother and Ala go out of the station hoping to buy some food. I sit myself on top of the bags wondering how we are going to find father in this mass of people. I am cold and agitated, my toes feel on fire and are so terribly itchy that, in spite of my tiredness, I take off my shoes, unwrap the layers of rags and let my feet cool down a little. All my toes look purple and are very swollen, the shiny skin is almost bursting. A woman sitting next to me hands me a small bottle of paraffin. "I see that the Russian winter has left its mark on you, put the paraffin on, it helps", she says. I soak the rags in the paraffin and gently wrap them around my feet. At first the burning is so intense that a lit match put to the rags could not have made it feel worse, yet after a while the pain and throbbing subsides. Even so I am not able to relax. A whole hour has passed and mother and Ala are not back yet. I hope nothing has happened to them. I begin to worry and at that very moment I hear mother's voice behind me. "Barbara, turn around!" There is father, standing only a couple of feet away from me! For a split second I don't recognise him. He doesn't look as tall as I always remembered, and he is very thin; his sunken cheeks and slim arms are slightly suntanned. He is dressed in old, worn, khaki trousers and a khaki shirt whose wide-open neck reveals his protruding collar-bones, but the smiling blue eyes are still the same. Mother and Ala stand aside watching. As I am much taller now, and father I think has shrunk a little, with ease I throw my arms around his neck. Burning tears stream down my face. The crowded, noisy station ceases to exist; there is only father and me.

Not far from the station, in a shabby, dirty house, father has a room where he stays. The adjoining couple of rooms are converted into offices. There are a lot of men walking about. They look tired and unwell but they all have a look of urgency about them. They seem to be very busy directing, giving information, organising transports, supplying food for the starving and helping to bury those who, on their way to freedom, did not make it. Every person's name and the place where she or he came from is carefully recorded. The lists are endless. Once in father's room and with the door closed, we start talking. There is so much to say, so many questions and so many answers! Mother continuously wipes tears from her face. She is worried about father's legs; they are very swollen with bluish-red blotches all over them and big, weeping sores. "Nothing to worry about, I am lucky, very, very lucky!" father says, and for a while the smile disappears from his face, his light-blue eyes darken and have a strange far-away look about them. In a quiet composed voice father tells us how on the very first day of the occupation of Lvov he escaped death. "As you know, the situation was hopeless, the police were slaughtered. Shortly before the Red Army marched in, just in case, I acquired a postman's uniform which I carried with me in a small, flat briefcase. On that fatal day a large group of police officers and I were walking down the street, not far from the Headquarters. Suddenly gun fire opened up on us. Everyone else was killed, but miraculously all the bullets missed me. I dashed into the nearest doorway, ripped off my commissioner's uniform and put on the postman's outfit. I waited for a while and in a quiet moment sneaked out of the doorway. Soon I was caught and taken to prison. At the very beginning the K.G.B. thought I was just a postman, but very quickly they got to know my true identity." "What happened next?" Ala asks. "Next? Oh, we won't be talking about that now!" father says. He gets up from a chair and starts pacing up and down the room. With one hand he rubs his forehead and the hand is trembling. "One thing is certain, they had their plans for me", he adds.

Next day mother, Ala and I sit in father's small room attempting to relax. Several days' old dirt, which accumulated on our bodies during the nightmarish journey, has been scrubbed away in a large, chipped bowl standing in a corner of the room. My long hair, thoroughly washed with a grey, gritty soap, feels crisp and clean. I try not to think of the countless nits which still cake each strand and are soon bound to hatch. I have just eaten a large slice of brown bread and am quite content. A poignant anxiety about father's emaciated appearance, which kept me awake part of the night, is almost gone. He appears to be full of drive. But mother is sick with worry and thinks that only the force of circumstances keeps him going. Now he is somewhere at the Orenburg station in the thick of things, dealing with all sorts of problems.

Some of the arriving Poles are in a very grave condition. They are carried off the trains and laid on the platforms. If they are still alive in a couple of days time, they will join a transport which will take them farther south.

Father desperately tries to find his two brothers Stach and Adam who were also prisoners of war somewhere in Russia. Every time a train arrives at the station his hopes are raised. Every time, with feverish agitation, he scans the platforms making numerous inquiries, but until now his efforts have been fruitless. At the end of the second day of our meeting with father, he comes back to the room with a withered middle-aged man. "This man and Adam were inmates in a prison barrack", father says. The man stands behind father, not saying a word. His claw-like fingers tug nervously at a dirty scarf knotted under his chin and the black round eyes dart swiftly around the room. He licks his dry narrow lips and begins to stare at a piece of bread lying on the table. Mother offers him the bread and a small, already open, tin of sardines. Ala runs out of the room to get more boiling water to make tea. While eating he tells us that uncle Adam died in his arms. "I was the only one who looked after him when he was ill. To keep him warm I gave him my woollen vest and my jumper", he says, shivering. He wraps his long, skinny arms around himself as if to say that he is cold and in great need. By now mother is in a flood of tears. She starts searching her bag for some money to repay him for his kindness to uncle. However, father, despite the very sad news, seems to be more agitated than upset. He takes off his tatty old jumper, gives it to the man, and impatiently leads him out of the room. "I don't believe Adam is dead", father says on his return. "My policeman's intuition tells me that the man is an imposter and a part of his story is false. I bet he has swindled quite a few poor, vulnerable people before, and he is going to do it again."

Many weeks after this incident father and uncle Adam met at the Orenburg station. We learned about the nasty little man who, expecting my very sick uncle to die soon, took from him not only his jumper and scarf but also his shoes. Father's eldest brother Stach was killed in Katyn. This we learned several years after the war.

Chapter 16

We stay in Orenburg only for a couple of days. And as there is a special supply of food for every rolling point, father is able to give us a treat. He has some tinned meat, fish and bread. As father can't leave his post in Orenburg and there is no place for us to stay, we are to move to Aktyubinsk, a city about 230 kilometres away. To help us settle in, we travel there with father, and the insignia of colonel on the epaulettes of his khaki shirt enables us to find a room in a carriage in which several Russian officers are travelling. Although the train is very crowded we are able to sit on a hard bench facing two Russian majors. One of them starts a conversation with Ala. His soft cultured voice is so different from the harsh Russian language we know. I, sitting next to her, have my eyes fixed on a louse which is slowly crawling over his green uniform and towards his neck. I also notice that Ala gets very embarrassed and I think quite cross. She told me later she didn't know what to do because, although the Poles are supposed to be their friends now, the thought of the terrible injustice and overwhelming misery they brought to so many thousands of Poles stopped her answering his polite questions. By an amazing stroke of luck we meet mother's friend, John and Mark in Aktyubinsk. Together with them and two other young Polish women we rent a two-room flat in a large, dark and cold building. Three of us occupy the smaller room, while the other five settle in the larger room. The whole place is damp and dirty, but father says that we are very fortunate to be able to find this accommodation. Ala looks very happy and her usually pale cheeks are coloured. The reason for her excitement is John, who is very attentive and helps her to carry the luggage. Their constant togetherness upsets me quite a bit. As the days go by, Ala starts to ignore me very noticeably and hides her diary so well that, in spite of my thorough search, I can never find it.

Every couple of weeks father visits us in Aktyubinsk. He stays only a day. He gives us some money and food and tells us all the current news. He is not certain when we will be able to leave Russia as this enormous task of gathering thousands of people from every corner of this huge country involves a lot of money and hard work. He looks ill and very tired. He says that we should get ready to spend yet another winter in Russia.

My thoughts go back to Razin. I see little Jan choking on the thick black smoke. I pray to God that everybody has moved out of that cursed house in the ditch. Our winter clothes are in a lamentable state. Warm underwear is practically non-existent. We patch already-patched gloves, socks and scarves. My tattered winter coat is much too short for me, but it will have to do. The weather is getting very cold and Ala is not well. We think she is getting yet another sore throat. It soon becomes apparent that Ala has typhus. She has the characteristic rash on the front of her chest, abdomen and back of her hands and her temperature is very high. In spite of the fever she looks ghostly white and her breathing is fast and shallow. Mother doesn't leave her bedside. Day after day, night after night, she gives her sips of water and puts cold compresses on her burning forehead. One day, about a week after Ala became ill, John rushes into the flat gasping, his eyes full of fear. "I just saw the Health Inspectors in the building's corridors, they are taking away all the people who are ill with typhus into an isolation hospital!" he says with trembling lips. Mother, who is sitting by Ala's bed, becomes rigid, but only momentarily. "John, give me a hand with Ala. We are going to hide her and we haven't got a minute to waste!" she says, her voice icy cold and very determined. Mother and John carry Ala, who is semi-conscious, onto a bed in the larger room. While they are doing it, I get rid of a pot under the bed, compresses and a glass of water. Ala is completely covered by blankets and a pillow is lightly arranged over her face. John, Mark and I sit carefully on the edge of the bed, forcing a smile. With the first knock at the door, mother calmly opens it. Three Health Inspectors walk in. They look around at the room where we all are and peep into the little room. John tells me a joke and I start laughing hysterically. "We are all well", I hear mother say. My pretended laugh changes into a loud cry but by this time the Health Inspectors are gone. We carry Ala back to her bed and breath a sigh of relief. Thank God they are gone, as what we know of the local hospitals fills us with horror. Our relief is short-lived. After about two hours they are back, this time unexpectedly. Someone in the building must have known about Ala's illness and tipped them off. Their stern faces know no opposition. "An epidemic of typhus is spreading, we have to protect other citizens. It is a criminal offence to hide a person with a contagious disease!" they say. Outside the building an open cart lined with straw is waiting for Ala. It is 40°C below zero and a blizzard is raging. Mother collects the blankets from all the beds. She shakes so much that the blankets are falling onto the floor. A Russian man, the driver of the cart, carries Ala out while mother follows. We are left in the room numb with pain. Late at night mother comes back and to our great surprise Ala is back too, but now she is in a delirium. "If she has to die, let her die at home!" mother says sobbing. Apparently as soon as they arrived in the hospital mother was told to bathe Ala. The bathroom was filthy and the large window had no pane. It was so cold inside that water splashed on the floor froze immediately. Mother didn't wait to see the rest of the hospital. She made such a terrible scene that, to get rid of her, they let her take Ala back home. She found the driver of the cart and begged him to drive them back. I think Ala is dying; apart from typhus she now has broncho-pneumonia. Father is temporarily released from his duties in Orenburg and is staying with us. He has brought a young Polish doctor whom he met in Orenburg. The doctor gives Ala an injection to bring the fever down for a while; apart from this he has nothing else. He seems very concerned. Father and mother don't talk, they just look at each other with anguish. John sits quietly in the corner of the room, pretending to read a newspaper, his sad eyes staring at one corner of the page. I can't imagine being without Ala. We went through so much together and now, when we are almost out of Russia, is Ala to die? The second week of Ala's illness is nearing an end. Ala is in a coma and we are waiting for the crisis, which we pray should bring a fall in temperature. On the fifteenth day, Ala opens her green almond-shaped eyes and looks around. Mother and father are by her side. The young doctor looks tenderly at Ala and, wiping her perspiring forehead, announces that the worst is over. It is the first time I have seen him smile. However, Ala is not out of the woods yet; the dreaded complication of broncho-pneumonia is still with her. The doctor comes often and every time he brings with him some nourishing food: a few eggs, some butter or milk. I wonder where he gets these precious items, as most certainly the shops don't have such products. Mother nurses Ala back to health with complete dedication. Looking at her nursing Ala reminds me of my own illness some years ago, when I was only seven years old. I had rheumatic fever, a disease which very often leaves cardiac complications. For ten long weeks mother nursed me in bed. On the very last day our doctor, who had visited me daily, said to mother: "Madam, you are a born nurse. It is only due to your constant and excellent care that your daughter's heart has not been damaged." Ala improves from day to day and is allowed up. She still looks ill and her once thick shiny black hair is lifeless. As she is unable to stand up or walk by herself, she is supported by mother and John and they walk around the room a couple of times a day, to make her legs stronger. John runs from market to market and spends hours queuing in freezing weather to buy a chicken for mother to make a broth for Ala. One day he spends five hours queuing, but when at long last he gets to the counter he finds that all the chickens are gone. In desperation he takes his watch off and offers it to a woman who bought the last chicken. Such a profitable exchange of goods doesn't happen very often, so it is not surprising that the woman takes John's watch without hesitation and he has her chicken. I am most impressed by John's sacrifice as I know that the watch was his only valuable possession. A few years back on the day he passed his entrance examination to grammar school his parents gave it to him. Even during the hopelessly gloomy days in Kolhoz, where everyone suffered from an acute lack of food, John held on to his watch.

When Ala was well, we always used to queue for bread together. The hours spent outside the shops seemed to pass quicker. But now since she is still very weak and has a troublesome cough, I go by myself. Every time, just before I leave the house, mother inspects my clothing thoroughly, making sure I am warmly dressed and every time she wraps an extra woollen scarf around my already-covered head. "Don't stand still in the queue. Jump up and down and move your arms about", she cautions me.

The weather is extremely cold. Two hours have passed and now there are only about forty people in front of me. Another hour or so and I will get my bread. I continue jumping up and down as mother said, but my feet are numb, I can hardly feel them. A freezing blasting wind bites my nose and cheeks and it is beginning to snow. I am so preoccupied with the exercises to keep me warm that I don't notice our young doctor until he taps me on the shoulder. He asks how Ala is and hands me a piece of paper folded in four. "Please give it to your sister", he says and walks away. Without a second thought I spread open the paper and start reading. "My dearest Ala . . .". Large flakes of snow fall on the ink-written page and the letters begin to blur, I shake off the snow flakes and read another couple of sentences, suddenly realizing that I should never have even opened it. I stuff it in my pocket, leave the queue, and run home without any bread. I can't wait to see Ala. I am very upset; the doctor wants to marry her! It is ridiculous! He is twice her age! And what about John? At home I tell mother that the shop ran out of bread and, beckoning Ala out of the room, give her the crumpled letter. I am greatly relieved when Ala, after carefully reading it, starts laughing. The very first hearty laugh since her illness. "I scarcely know him. During most of his visits I was unconscious", she says. The following day I meet the doctor again outside the bread shop. To complete my mission as quickly as possible I hand him a note from Ala and, without waiting for him to read it, I position myself somewhere in the midde of the long queue, hoping no one has noticed my bold intrusion. But the people behind me start to grumble and shout; I am pushed off the pavement and I am forced to take my rightful place at the very end of the queue. I have a very nasty feeling that long before I reach the counter all the bread will be gone.

Father goes back to Orenburg but, as Christmas is only a couple of weeks away, he will be back soon. On Christmas Eve, before supper, we break and eat tiny pieces of blessed wafers, wishing each other good health. This time not only mother but we all cry and the tears are tears of joy that once again we are together. By now Ala has recovered completely and I don't think she realizes how gravely ill she was. She even tells me that she didn't mind having typhus as the extra attention and care John showed her during and after her illness was very enjoyable. Now she is fretting that soon John will have to join the army and she might never see him again.

Thank goodness winter is almost over. Father tells us that soon we and the several thousands of Poles will be travelling farther south to other rallying points. Although the news is good we are now very worried about mother. She is very lethargic and wants to sleep all the time. Every joint in her legs and arms is swollen and painful. A muscle in her left calf is wasting and the affected leg looks much thinner. Ala's and my aggravation is heightened by the fear that once again father will come with the same young doctor who looked after Ala. We breath a sigh of relief when father arrives with a complete stranger. The doctor doesn't know what the trouble is, but points out that the dampness and the cold of the room is the predominating factor in her illness. Mother has to stay in bed and the wasted muscle in her leg is to be massaged daily. He shows Ala and me how to do it. After a few weeks mother improves, but her leg still looks much slimmer. The doctor assures us that though it is going to take a long time, mother's leg will eventually get back to normal.

I am getting very restless. Why are we still here? Why does it take so long to leave Russia? We hear of so many tragedies. The people's hopes of freedom and reunion with their loved ones are shattered by disease and death. Father witnesses the most heart-breaking scenes on the Orenburg's station platforms. Some nights I wake up terrified that something will happen and we might not make it. Yesterday John left Aktyubinsk to join the army. Ala looks miserable and though she doesn't admit it, I know she has been crying. Our small flat seems so quiet now; I miss John's jokes and Ala's happy laughter. Soon after John's departure his mother becomes ill. She has a fever and is sick. We pray it is not typhus. Mark too is not well, both his knees are very swollen and he can hardly walk. We are very worried. Who will look after them, as our turn has come to leave Aktyubinsk? "What will happen to our friends?" mother anxiously asks. But father is very determined, insisting that we must go now and a spark of steel in his usually gentle eyes says more than his words. He assures us that there will be another transport which our friends will join. The two young women who are sharing the flat are also staying behind. This relieves our minds a little as they will be able to look after John's mother and Mark. Father too is staying in Orenburg; his job is not finished yet, but he is hoping to join us soon.

The night before we leave I have a nightmare. I dream that I am in a long narrow tunnel at the end of which a very faint light flickers. I am attempting to crawl forwards to reach the light, but I am not making any progress. Layers of extraordinary big grey lice are obstructing my way. It seems that all the lice from Burlaghaz and Razin are here and they start creeping all over my body. I scream and wake up in a cold sweat. My thumb and the forefinger of my right hand are tightly pressed together; the knuckles are white. I loosen the grip and I see a squashed dead louse falling down onto my pillow.

Chapter 17

It is Spring 1942. An old goods train is taking hundreds of us to Dzhala Abad, a town in Kirgizia. It is supposed to be our last stop before we leave the Soviet Union through Krasnovodsk and the Caspian sea. The journey is long and tiring and the train crowded, yet the general atmosphere is one of elation. A group of young people in our carriage sings; Ala and I join in. Mother sits in a corner of the carriage talking to an elderly woman. Above the jolly words of a song I can clearly hear mother's voice: "Hope and desire to live is the most wonderful tonic and the best medicine there is. Just look at this train. We are all stricken by poverty and illness, the majority of us have lost relatives and friends, our dearest and nearest, yet we are smiling and are able to sing." Every time the train stops we are confronted with people, mostly children, begging for food or money. Their mongol, sad faces are very appealing; we know what hunger means. Although now we are not starving, we have nothing to give. At some station we see huge mountains of rotting grain guarded by soldiers. If only this grain could be given to the starving millions before it rots completely.

We stop for many hours in Tashkent, a city on the border of Uzbekistan and Kirgizia. We are told that on no account must we leave the train, as the travellers are made to use filthy communal bath-houses where they are 'deloused'. A group of people in white overalls are searching the carriages and the platforms; they are looking for the ill who have typhus. Once the sick are rounded up, they are put into an awaiting lorry and taken to an isolation hospital. Some of the victims of the overzealous and overworked Health Inspectors are only suffering from a bad bout of flu. As the officials are in a hurry, a quick diagnosis is often incorrect. Those who are not well are truly terrified of being taken away; they hide in dark corners or under benches. A family next to us is frantically trying to hide their four-year-old son. "Quickly, quickly!" the man says. With trembling hands he tips out the contents of their old, battered suitcase and stuffs the little boy inside. The boy looks ill and his laboured breathing is very wheezy. I am afraid that his dry, violent cough will give him away. "My God, if they find my son and take him and us off this train, that will be our end! We will never get out of Russia", the boy's father says. Meanwhile the boy's mother gathers the scattered belongings from the floor, ties them up into a bundle and sits on top of them. She looks terribly downhearted. Mother tries to console her. But what comfort can one give to a mother who has already lost two of her children? Thank God 'the angels of mercy' are pushed for time and their search is not very thorough.

In Dzhala Abad and all around it a couple of divisions of the partly-formed Polish army and their families are settled waiting for the next move.

We rent a small room from a Russian family on the outskirts of town. From the very first day we notice that our jolly and friendly landlady is afraid of her two teenage children, in particular her sixteen-year-old son Nicholas. Whenever we say anything which is not in line with Communist thinking or Stalin's régime she looks around in fear and, if one of her children is there, she abruptly changes the subject. Her children, like all young people in the Soviet Union, are brought up to believe that 'Father Stalin' and his rules are the saviours of the people. Those whose ideas are different are the enemies of the Soviet Union and deserve to be punished. Hard labour camps are the usual places where the ungrateful citizens are banished for several years, and if they happen to be your own parents it is just too bad. Nicholas is very arrogant and sure of himself. Yesterday I almost had a fight with him. I have a small, faded picture of Jesus and Mary, and in every place we stay, I get it out of my bag and fix it above my bed; I do the same here. As soon as Nicholas sees the picture, he walks over to my bed, roughly tears it off the wall and says with irony: "You should know better than that, it is Stalin you should be praying to!" I am stunned by his action but only momentarily. With an urge to kill I jump at him screaming. Thank goodness mother walks in and grasps the situation at once. Silently she picks up the crumpled picture and pulling me by my hand, leads me out of the room. "Haven't you learned anything, Barbara? We are only one step away from freedom, so control yourself!" she says in a quivering whisper. Soon after this incident we learn that Nicholas is now old enough to join the Red Army. We greet the news with joy and relief, and I suspect that his mother shares our feelings.

It is midsummer now. The rallying point in Orenburg is liquidated, and father is with us once again. The weather is incredibly hot and the sun so intense that walking about during the day is almost unbearable. In spite of this, the natives are dressed in thick sheepskin coats, the women wear long, loose trousers and their faces are covered by veils. At night our room gets so stuffy and hot that we move our beds outside into an apricot orchard, not far from the house. These nights I will never forget.

Four narrow wooden beds stand side-by-side under the apricot trees. My bed is next to father's. We can't sleep; after a sweltering day this is the best time. The stillness, like the starry sky above us, is immense. Father's low, quiet voice is very soothing. He is telling me a story, a real story. His passionate love and hobby is history. He knows so many historical facts of so many nations: their kings and heroes, their battles, victories and defeats, their glory and shame. Tonight he is telling me about the Polish kings, right from the very beginning, from the year 966 AD. I fall asleep in the middle of the battle of Grunvald. The nights are father's escape from reality. While talking his sunken eyes are closed. The burden of the past two years, which is so very evident during the day, vanishes from his face. Reality is still very grave.

In Kermine, a place not far from Dzhala Abad, where the majority of Poles are gathered, the situation is deplorable. It is a valley of death. The people who, with their last surge of strength, travel thousands of miles from Siberia, Arkhangelsk, Kolyma, Kazakhstan and other places are dying of typhus and dysentery on the doorstep to freedom. Hospitals and barracks converted into hospital wards are overflowing with the dying. The grave-diggers can't keep up. The corpses are buried in communal graves without coffins. In Dzhala Abad the situation is not so tragic, but the longer we stay here, the worse it will become. The first transport of Poles from Dzhala Abad, Kermine and the surrounding areas has already departed to Krasnovodsk, a port on the Caspian sea, the very last stop before leaving Russia. We are to wait for the next transport and be in readiness. There is no talk of going back to Poland. The war is raging and Europe now is a hell.

"I am so glad I have two daughters", mother says. "If Ala was a boy she would be in the Polish forces now, getting ready to fight the Germans." But Ala does want to join the Polish Women's Auxiliary Unit and is very determined about it. Every day she pesters mother as to why she is not allowed to join when a lot of girls her age are already in it. Mother is unyielding and tells her that the matter is closed and she doesn't want to discuss it any longer. The thought of Ala in soldier's uniform amuses me a little because she still looks very frail after her illness. I suspect the real reason is not her willingness to do a noble deed, but the hope of meeting John. To cheer her up, I tell her to stop brooding, because here in Dzhala Abad are plenty of young Polish soldiers and I have noticed that they all stare at her. Ala looks at me with disgust and once again tells me that I am silly. I am really very pleased to be only twelve years old and not have to have all the problems my sister has.

Today we go to a very solemn mass celebrated by a Polish bishop. The altar is in an open field and beautifully decorated with white and red flowers. A brand new Polish flag flutters in the hot wind. The soldiers line up on both sides of the altar. The very patriotic sermon is full of hope and encouragement. "Soon you will be fighting for your country, for a free Poland. God be with you!" the bishop says in a clear and strong voice, blessing the soldiers and the huge crowd. We all start sobbing. The whole ceremony is very moving and uplifting. Afterwards the bishop confirms a whole congregation of young people, Ala and I included.

In Dzhala Abad is a big market where one can sell old clothing. As rumours spread that we will be going to Africa, mother decides to sell all our tattered winter clothes, hoping that the rumours are true and we won't be needing them any more. My old, darned woollen gloves are the last items to go.

They are just about to be sold to a Russian woman, when I suddenly get an urge to keep them. These old gloves not only remind me of two frightful winters, but more importantly of the excitement and guilt I felt when hiding stolen grain inside them. We were in Razin at the time and Ala's job was to clean the village warehouse. I used to visit Ala many times during the day. As most of the time I was hungry, the walk and Ala's company helped me to take my mind off food. One part of the warehouse was stocked with sacks of grain. While Ala was busy sweeping the threshing floor, I made a tiny hole in one of the sacks through which some of the golden corn spilled out. I gathered the corn quickly, stuffing it inside my gloves. I vividly remember the agitation and overwhelming guilt which I felt walking past the warehouse's watchman who was sitting by the door. I made countless trips to and fro and every time I passed the watchman I smiled sweetly at him. I hid my stolen grain from mother and Ala but, after a week when I had about one kilo, I told them it was given to me. After soaking some of it overnight, mother cooked it. It was sweet with a full flavour, nothing like the bitter bran flour we were getting. Recently, just before my confirmation, I went to confession. I told the priest my sin but I am almost sure he couldn't have heard me clearly because I was not reprimanded or given a penance.

Chapter 18

At the very beginning of August, the second transport leaves for Krasnovodsk, and we are to go now. However, mother wants to stay, as father is very ill and hospitalised. He begs her from his hospital bed not to delay the departure. "Think of our daughters, they have a right to live and be free; the quicker you get out of here, the better!" he says. So we pack our bags and leave. The journey in the goods train lasts three days. As with the previous journey to Dzhala Abad, the train is swarmed with women and children at almost every station. They look poor and undernourished – just like us. They beg for food and clothing. We smile and wave but have nothing to give them. I feel painfully embarrassed and persistently pester mother that we should give them something. "If you feel so generous, take your skirt off and give it away", mother finally says, very annoyed with my unreasonable demand. The thought of being skirtless soon shuts me up.

I wish the train wouldn't stop at the stations for such a long time; the sight of these deprived people distresses me. One very young girl tugs at her mother's hand crying loudly. In between the sobs she seems to be repeating the same words over and over. To hear her words more clearly, I lean out of the open window. "I want Mama!" I hear her cry in Polish. Well, it is a miracle that I did not fall out of the window head first. I think I have Ala to thank for that as she grabbed my legs at the last minute. The little girl joins the group of orphans who are travelling in our train. It seems her parents died on their way from Siberia to one of the rallying points in the south. A Russian woman took pity on her and looked after her for several weeks. But one more mouth to feed is an extra burden so, as soon as she learned that a train full of Polish people was stopping at a nearby station, she took the girl with her, assuming rightly that the child would be able to join the transport.

We arrive on the Krasnovodsk beach very early in the morning to wait for the boats. Though it is only dawn it is already hot and the beach, which is a mixture of pebbles and coarse sand, is filthy. Heaps of rubbish, tar and large greasy patches of oil cover it almost entirely. Everyone, and there are thousands of us, flops on top of their belongings, full of expectations that very soon the boats, which are to take us across the Caspian sea to Pahlavi, will start arriving.

Hours pass by and it gets dreadfully hot. We feel sluggish and sweat trickles down our faces in big, shiny drops. There is no shade at all, nowhere to hide. Those who are ill get worse. Drinking water is unobtainable. Some people, already dehydrated through long illness, crawl to the edge of the sea, eagerly drinking the smelly, oily sea water. As soon as they swallow it they are violently sick. Everyone has a burning desire to drink. Water is as precious as gold in this port. There is no supply of fresh water in Krasnovodsk. It is delivered daily in huge containers to the people who live here. Soon the locals take advantage of our pathetic situation. They come with buckets of tepid, cloudy water and start selling it at exorbitant prices. Mother gives away our only quilt for two glasses of water. A woman next to us pulls off her wedding ring for one glass of water for her sick daughter. An old man takes off his only pair of shoes and with shaking hands grabs a small cup of water, trembling so much that he spills it all on the dry beach. I see a small girl of about eight carrying one very large water melon. I don't know where she got the melon from but before she reaches her family a teenage boy snatches the melon from her and disappears into the crowd. At last, we see two soldiers pulling a cart with two, very big barrels full of water. Before the soldiers have time to stop and start distributing it, the crowd of thirsty people craving for a drink rushes towards the cart, pushing and fighting. The two barrels of highly-valued drink overturn and their contents quickly soak into the dirty sand.

The first old, rusty cargo boat arrives the next day very late in the afternoon. The tired, apathetic crowd stirs. Children have priority and there are several hundred of them. The orphans are organised into small groups to be looked after by adults. They start to board the boat. I look at them with misty eyes. They look like skeletons. To keep lice at bay, their heads are closely shaven. Although they are all very young, their faces and large sad eyes are old. I feel sick at heart, they are such a sorry sight. Yet there are people who try to push their way before the children, they shout and argue with the organisers. Some scenes are very unpleasant and shameful. It seems that illness, heat and thirst disturbed their minds. The eagerness to get on the boat and leave this country is so great that, for some, human decency does not exist.

After a couple of hours complete darkness falls upon the beach. The second boat arrives and we embark at long last. The organisers check and re-check the names, making sure that the right people get on the right boat, but the task is hopeless. The boat is so full that I seriously think it might sink. Every free space on the decks is taken by people and immediately a long queue forms outside the solitary, filthy toilet. With a tide of people pushing us from behind we reach the top deck. We find standing room among some big, wooden containers and huge reels of thick rope smudged with tar. The night is pitch black, I can't see anything, but my feet are sliding in all directions and the smell is awful. I suggest to mother that we should move but by now the deck is so crammed with people that it is out of the question. We are extremely tired but can't sleep standing up. The boat creaks and sways and though we are on the top deck we can distinctly hear the noise of the engine. With the first rays of light we see with revulsion that we had placed our luggage in a pool of vomit. I begin to shiver and retch, I want to run to the railings and be sick overboard but the wall of human bodies blocks my way. I firmly put both hands over my mouth. Mother sees my green face and bulging eyes, but there is nothing she can do. I am sick all over Ala's skirt and am thankful that for the last twenty-four hours I had very little to eat.

We reach Pahlavi, a port in Iran, the following night. We are finally out of the Soviet Union. It is 11th August 1942.

Chapter 19

The boat anchors about a mile from shore. We board smaller boats which take us right into the port, where several lorries are waiting for us. After a short boat ride we unload on the flat, sandy Pahlavi beach in 'the dirty camp'. From now on our journeys and camps are organised by the English. The Pahlavi beach is entirely taken over by long rows of sheds with open sides. The roofs of these sheds look like huge raffia mats supported at each corner by tall poles firmly secured in the sand. The only function of these sheds is to provide shade. The weather is extremely hot and the fine, golden sand feels on fire. I am a little worried about how I am going to walk bare-footed, as I threw my shabby, sickly-smelling sandals into the sea. Every time I venture out of the shade my feet get scorched. Mother, as always, has a solution to my dilemma. She tears an old towel into two halves and now I hop around the camp like a kangaroo. I spread a piece of towel in front of me and hop, then another piece and hop. I quite enjoy it and see a lot of children and some adults who are engaged in exactly the same jumping exercises. Unfortunately I can't keep up with Ala who now walks much quicker than she usually does. When we go down to the sea she practically runs and is already in the water while I am only half-way there. I think she does this merely to annoy me.

We are not hungry any more, but our diet is lamentable. Three times a day, every day, we get pressed, nauseatingly sweet dates: dates morning, noon and night, for breakfast, lunch and supper. I wonder where all these dates are coming from to feed so many hungry mouths; somewhere the harvest must have been exceptionally good. I vouch never to eat dates again once we leave Pahlavi. Apart from dates we get very greasy soup, thick with overcooked rice and full of big gristly lumps of mutton fat. Everybody warns everybody else not to eat too much from this delectable menu as our starved stomachs won't be able to digest it. A lot of ill people, especially those with dysentery, are still in a very dangerous situation. Our shed adjoins the orphanage where emaciated children slowly eat the very greasy rice soup or nibble at dates. Some feel so sick that they can't eat it. I see them slowly shuffle to the makeshift toilets which are scattered about the camp. Their bare, stick-like legs tremble and, to my amazement, are insensitive to the hot sand.

After one week in 'the dirty camp' our turn has come to be cleaned. We collect our clothes and form a queue outside a large tent at the side of the camp. The men are separated from the women. Before we enter the tent, we undress and leave our clothes at the entrance. The heaps of dirty, lice-ridden clothes are later burned. We walk inside completely naked. Several showers are fixed to the roof of the tent which holds about thirty women and children. Before we start washing, the women are given razors and are asked to shave everywhere. Our heads are closely inspected and if the lice and nits haven't taken them over entirely the hair can stay. Thanks to mother's dedicated care I can keep my plaits. A few young English soldiers mingle with the naked women adjusting the flow of water. I feel very embarrassed, but the majority of women don't care. They are immensely happy to be able to have a cool, long shower and wash their sweaty bodies thoroughly with carbolic-smelling soap. I have noticed that being only twelve years old and not quite grown up is a blessing in this situation. We are handed small, rough towels for drying and before we leave the tent 'new' clothes are given to us. Each of us gets one set of underwear, one dress, one scarf and one handkerchief. Those who have no shoes at all get one pair of ill-fitting sandals or plimsolls. I get a pair of brown plimsolls, two sizes too big for me. I tie the long laces around my ankles making sure not to lose my precious footwear. Ala moans that her dress has a patch on the shoulder and is much too long. Mother's bright red dress with large yellow flowers is hilarious; every time we look at her we burst out laughing. Once we get rid of the lice we are promoted to 'the clean camp', which consists of exactly the same accommodation and is some distance away from 'the dirty camp'.

We are also given pocket money. These donations of money and second-hand clothing are very unpleasant and embarrassing; in a way we feel like beggars, but we have no choice. "We will pay for it dearly", I hear people say. I didn't realize then that the payment would be high and in young men's blood.

We use our money to buy some ice cream and fruit. Mother allows herself some extravagant spending; she buys a packet of cigarettes. While in Russia she smoked very little. The tobacco she was sometimes able to obtain was very coarse, sharp and strong and, as there was no cigarette paper, she had to roll it in a piece of old newspaper which made it taste even worse. Some people smoked dry, finely-chopped beetroot leaves. Mother tried it a couple of times but had no enjoyment from it. Now she is smoking a long Persian cigarette and I think she relishes its taste but feels a little guilty. "I should really give it up, it is such a waste of money", she says.

Two days after our move to 'the clean camp', father arrives on the Pahlavi beach with a group of officers and soldiers. He looks very bad, his legs are even more swollen now. He tells us that the day we left for Krasnovodsk he became so ill that he started to lose hope of ever seeing us again. The doctor who attended him during his illness was very much against his imminent journey. "If I had stayed in Dzhala Abad for another day and listened to his advice, I would be dead by now", father says. He is with us for only a few days. A large contingent of soldiers is moving to Iraq and then on to Egypt, and father is going with them. He says goodbye to us on the beach. He holds on to the shed's pole, shaking. I fear that if he lets go of the pole he will collapse.

Our prolonged stay in Pahlavi makes us very impatient. "How much longer?" This question is on everyone's lips. We are almost accustomed to the gritty feel of sand in our rice soup. The sticky dates are covered in it. The fine, golden sand gets everywhere. One morning at about 3.00 a.m., after almost four weeks in Pahlavi, alarms get us up from our sandy beds. We are to be ready by 8.00 a.m. At last we are leaving Pahlavi!! We are going to another camp in Teheran and the lorries are waiting for us.

At first, for no apparent reason, the long column of lorries loaded with people stops every few kilometres. "If this is how we are going to travel, it will take a week to reach Teheran", we say. But this crawling exercise soon changes into a race. Our young Iranian driver knows no fear. With a devilish smile on his handsome face, he presses the accelerator at the most dangerous places, overtaking other lorries on sharp bends. A narrow treacherously winding road climbs up through the rocky mountains and then descends steeply. The view is breathtaking if only we could enjoy it! Mother feels sick and keeps her eyes tightly closed. We nudge her from time to time and point at the magnificent mountains, rushing streams or wide rivers far away in the distance, but she doesn't want to see anything, she just wants to get to Teheran in one piece. The lorry swerves from side to side or drives on the very edge of the road, only inches away from a sheer drop of several hundred feet; the ravines below seem bottomless. Ala and I hold on tightly to the sides of the lorry and we too feel a little scared when, at top speed, our driver overtakes army vehicles, which it seems he can't bear in front of him. In sign language some people try to persuade our young driver to slow down a little, but to no avail. He laughs heartily seeing our fear. We stop in Qazviin for the night, after eleven hours of reckless driving. During our journey we saw four completely mangled lorries at the bottom of the ravines, one of which we learned later was full of Polish women and children. The second leg of our journey is just as hair-raising. After a good night's sleep our driver's untamed desire for speed has increased. We resign our lives to fate. Miraculously we reach Teheran late that night.

Chapter 20

Four sprawling camps surround the city. Our camp is seven kilometres from Teheran and its location is idyllic. Huge tents squat among beautiful bushes full of blossom, tall vividly green trees provide shade and crystal clear streams trickle down little rocks on both sides of narrow, winding roads. Luckily our camp's site is the most pleasant one, the other three are situated in old army barracks or an old factory. I wander alone around this lovely park and look at the exotic flowers, admiring the variety of their shapes and colours. Though it is getting dark I don't want to go back to our tent which holds sixty-five people. The thought of it makes me shiver, as there is never a quiet moment with so many of us in one tent. Happiness, laughter, crying, moaning or anger, all these emotions mixed together form a continuous background to our everyday life. For so many months now we have roamed from place to place, always in a large, poverty-stricken crowd. I yearn to be by myself just for a while. Although I see a lot of people walking about, not far away from me, and the tops of our tents are clearly visible, I pretend that I am alone and on holiday in Poland, in the mountain region of Zakopane and, instead of cypress trees, tall pine trees grow around me. I have a full basket of wild mushrooms and feel very excited at the prospect of showing them proudly to my parents. My day-dreaming is interrupted by Ala who sees me sitting under a tree and tells me to go back to our tent as mother is worried about what has happened to me.

Recently mother has not been well. She is very weak and is losing weight. It seems that the two years in Russia, fighting for survival and providing food for us, drained all her energy. The extreme worry about father's health makes matters worse. We hope to stay in Teheran for a longer period of time so mother can get some of her strength back. Thankfully the camp conditions here are good in comparison to Pahlavi. Although we sleep on the ground and countless flies and other nameless insects keep us awake at night, the washing facilities are adequate. We can have a hot or cold shower every day and we have soap. The laundry where we can wash our clothes is set up in one of the tents and there is even an iron, a most unexpected luxury.

Everyone gets some money and more clothes. In addition to these, each of us receives a mug, plate, spoon, knife and fork, comb and toothbrush. We feel very rich. With money in our pockets Ala, two friends and I decide to venture out of the camp and visit Teheran. Now, whenever Teheran is mentioned during a conversation, the vision of a fabulously wealthy, beautiful suburban part of the city flashes in front of my eyes, as this is the part which the four of us unknowingly enter.

Magnificent pastel coloured villas with intricate arches supported by tall pillars hide behind exotic and perfectly kept gardens. Shimmering fountains and emerald swimming pools add to the tranquility of the surroundings. For a while we wander around in a daze, not knowing that this is only one very small part of this city and that the other parts are very different. As the day is hot and we are very thirsty, we find a small but exclusive looking street and, entering a restaurant, ask for iced coffee. Each of us gets a tall, crystal glass full of strong and very aromatic coffee with delicious creamy ice cream floating on top. It tastes heavenly! Our enjoyment is short lived as we find that between the four of us we haven't got enough money to pay for one glass of coffee, let alone four. We are overwhelmed with embarrassment. Ala's cheeks become crimson red, one of the friends is almost crying. A lack of common language is worst of all. Ala has a brain-wave and starts the difficult conversation in her elementary French, promising the young waiter to bring the rest of the money tomorrow. The waiter either understands her brave attempts to explain the delicate situation or just has no concern for his boss's loss, because he waves us goodbye with a friendly smile. We get a lift back to the camp in an army vehicle. During our three week stay in the camp we tried several times to find this fairy-tale district and the little coffee shop, but we never succeeded.

Today Ala and I are going to the neighbouring camp whose accommodation is a large old factory. We just heard that little Jan and his mother are staying there. Jan is a big boy now and he greets us with outstretched arms. We are very happy that they too are out of Kazakhstan. But our happiness is marred by other heart-rending news. My friend in Razin, a girl of my age, is dead and her mother and younger brother are still there. I begin to realise that there are still several thousands of Poles left all over the Soviet Union, thousands who may never get out, and we are the lucky ones. Jan's mother tells us the most devastating story. The train on which they were travelling to the port of Krasnovodsk collided with a huge oil cistern. The very first carriages, where the orphans were travelling, derailed and crashed into a deep ditch. Two children were killed and several seriously injured. They lay amongst twisted metal and shattered glass. Some moaned in pain, some cried, some lay motionless and unconscious. The occupants of the rear carriage, who apart from being shocked were unharmed, almost immediately started to treat the casualties. Sheets were torn into long strips serving as bandages, towels were used to stop the bleeding, and pieces of wood from the mangled carriages were used as splints to support broken bones. When the distant sound of ambulance sirens reached their ears, in panic they gathered the injured orphans and hid them in their carriages. To allow the children to be taken to a hospital and be left behind in Russia seemed unthinkable. The children would be lost forever. The ambulance crew was told that the children suffered only minor injuries. They collected two small bodies and left. Then when we meet Mark in a group of orphans our spirits are completely broken. Mark looks ill and is limping, his once bushy blond hair is shaven, his very unsteady walk makes him look old. Crying openly he tells us that to save his live he was taken into an orphanage and crossed the border with all the other parentless children. His mother was too ill to travel. "I should never have left her, I don't know if she is still alive", he says quietly. On the way back to our camp we hardly talk, we are very upset and have every intention not to tell mother all the bad news at once; she has been feeling very low the last few days. Ala wonders if

John, who is in Iraq now, knows about his mother's fate, as letters can only be sent through the military post which seems to be very unreliable and delays are long, owing to censorship. More than anything else, our meeting with Mark casts a dark shadow over me. During a sleepless night I try to put myself in Mark's place, but my imagination fails me. Oh God, how lucky we are!

Here in Teheran, apart from the mini clinics which every camp has for minor cases, is a big hospital set up in an old Iranian military barracks, just outside the city. The hospital is run by Polish doctors and nurses. All of them work non-stop and can hardly keep up with the constant flow of ill people. Patients with malnutrition, typhus, double pneumonia, dysentery and a variety of other serious diseases fill the makeshift wards to overflowing. Every corridor and every corner of the old barracks is taken over by the sick; some have beds, some don't. Today mother and Ala are going to visit a friend in the big hospital. By rights the friend should now be lying among all the other Poles in the big Polish cemetery outside Teheran. The story of her remarkable survival is told to us by her twelve year old daughter Sophie.

Sophie's mother became ill during the journey from Pahlavi to Teheran. As soon as they arrived in the camp she was taken into hospital. Typhus was diagnosed. As the days went by her condition became more and more grave. Sophie visited her daily. For hours she sat on the edge of the bed looking at the deathly pale face of her unconscious mother. There were moments when she was unsure whether her mother was still alive, so shallow was her breathing. One day, when Sophie entered the familiar hospital ward, her heart missed a beat; someone else was occupying her mother's bed. Stammering with fear, she asked a nurse where her mother was. "She was taken to the mortuary an hour ago", the nurse said, pointing in its direction. Sophie ran to the mortuary, she had to see her mother for the last time. Tears blinded her as, gasping, she entered the large room whose floor was covered with bodies wrapped up in white sheets, all lined up neatly side by side and all looking alike. To look for her would be a full day's job and time was short as all the bodies had to be buried promptly as the weather is very hot. The mortuary attendant pointed at the body nearest to the entrance. Sophie, demented with grief, fiercely ripped the sheet off her mother's face and threw herself over her body. With her ear next to her mother's chest she heard a faint heart beat and while kissing the deathly white face, she felt the warmth of her very shallow breath. The realisation that her mother was alive struck her like lightning. She became hysterical and screamed to have her mother taken back to the ward. The mortuary attendant called a nurse, the nurse called a sister and the sister called a doctor. Sophie's mother was taken back to the ward where she improved and was now on her way to complete recovery. Mother and Ala are taking her a big bunch of flowers.

Sometimes Ala annoys me immensely. For example, today she told mother about the small teaching groups which are being formed in all the camps, and points out that I should attend them. As there are a lot of children of school age here who have not been to school for two and a half years, those whose profession was teaching before the war are getting very concerned about our young minds. With dedication worthy of their noble profession, they gather the children around them and, sitting under the trees, begin to teach. No blackboards, no books, no paper. I have known about these teaching sessions for a while now, but see no reason to join or tell mother about them. Mother, of course, wholeheartedly agrees with Ala. "Why aren't you joining these classes?" I ask Ala. However, Ala, in her patronising voice which always irritates me greatly, announces that advanced courses have not been formed yet.

We now know for certain that we will be going to East Africa and English will be very helpful. With some money which father recently sent us Ala buys a small book: 'English for Beginners'. Looking through it with interest she comments that this language has the most peculiar pronunciation and she doesn't think she will ever master it.

Chapter 21

Unfortunately our stay in Teheran is nearing its end. We have been here now for more than three weeks. A lot of people, mainly the sick and their families, are remaining in the camp, but we have to move on. We are going to Ahvaz by train, leaving behind the magical view of the Elburz mountains. By now we are used to so many inconveniences that the train which provides adequate seating accommodation for everyone is greatly appreciated. At night we arrange ourselves in such a fashion that we can stretch our legs, but sleeping is almost impossible. Our train goes through countless, winding, long tunnels. We are told that from Teheran to Ahvaz there are one hundred and forty five of them. The train sways like a small boat on a rough sea and, as the windows have to be closed while we pass through the tunnels, it gets very hot and stuffy inside. During the day we admire the view; the magnificent imposing mountains are so dominating that they are almost frightening. After two days of travelling we arrive in Ahvaz. We walk two kilometres to the camp while our baggage goes by lorry. Our lodgings are huge, very high horse stables, which hold several hundred of us. A stable again! And I thought that after Burlaghaz I would never live in a stable again.

For me Ahvaz means cockroaches. Those repugnant creatures are about two inches long and look like giants in comparison to those of Burlaghaz or Razin. Our presence doesn't bother them at all. On the contrary, they start coming out in hoards from all the cracks in the brick walls and cement floors. Those voracious beetle-like insects infest our bags and boxes. I am astounded by their hyperactivity and, although they are supposed to be nocturnal creatures, during the day they crawl all over us just as much. With every step I take the grinding noise of squelched cockroaches rings in my ears.

The weather is very hot and the strong wind blows dust and dirt from the smelly street right into the stables. Clouds of dust linger around for most of the day. The water we get in the big buckets is slimy and warm and we are very cautious about what we eat as the food we get doesn't look very fresh. Hoards of big horseflies are our constant companions.

Mother coughs day after day, night after night. Someone tells us that juice from raw onions is an excellent medicine for coughs. Ala buys a couple of kilos of onions in a nearby market, chops them finely and squeezes the juice through a piece of fine cloth. Mother drinks a couple of spoonfuls of this smelly liquid three times a day. But after two days she has to discontinue the treatment as the strong smell of onion is so unpleasant that people around us start to complain. Only one night we sleep in the stables, the following nights the majority of us move out and sleep outside on the pavements. We would rather have people walking over us than the giant cockroaches. Iranian soldiers who, for our safety patrol the stables, don't mind at all. They smile in a friendly way and seem to understand. A young English officer, whose duty is to see that everything is in order, visits us regularly now. He brings biscuits, sweets and soap. The soap is the only thing mother can't resist taking, but the biscuits and sweets she stubbornly refuses. Ala, with the help of her little book, tries to make conversation. The whole situation is very amusing. He talks very quickly and we can't distinguish any words. Ala, on the other hand pronounces every word very slowly and exactly the way it is written. "I wish he would stop visiting us!" Ala says one day. "It is very frustrating to see a blank expression on his face while I do my best to entertain him. He has no imagination at all!" One day our English friend brings a small notebook with him and asks Ala to write something in it. Without a second thought, and to my great amazement, Ala writes: "A friend in need is a friend indeed". She admits later that this is the only verse she has learned by heart and thinks it is the most suitable in the circumstances. The day we leave Ahvaz he comes to say goodbye and this time at last mother accepts a large box of sweets from him. While talking he points at his forehead, his mouth and his eyes to say that he will think about us, but won't have anyone to talk to or look at, and as always he looks only at Ala. My observation of his behaviour forces me to tell Ala that he is deeply in love with her. "He is much too old for me, he must be at least twenty-two years old!" she says laughing.

Among the thousands of us are a lot of clever and talented people whose spirit and creativity has not been suppressed. There are musicians, actors, painters, dancers and especially teachers. At every stopping place they come forward, anxious about us, the children. "We are the future of the nation," they say. "No matter what the conditions are, our spirits and minds must not be neglected!" Therefore it is decided that even here, in sweltering dirty Ahvaz we are to entertain our English hosts. A group of children who don't look very emaciated and I are to dance and sing Polish folk songs. As we don't have the national costumes our 'Pahlavi-style' dresses will have to do. The stage is set in an old army barrack and a battered piano, completely out of tune, is played by one of the organisers. The performance is such a success that we are to repeat it in a couple of days, as some more English officials are coming to visit the camp.

I haven't got the slightest ambition to be a performer and I get very nervous but, to my surprise, I enjoy it tremendously. Our English audience distributes sweets among the children, they smile, clap their hands and altogether are very polite. We soon learn that using the French or German language as a means of communication with our guests is useless; the English speak only English. The more adventurous ones struggle unavailingly with more complicated Polish surnames. However, thanks to some of our organisers whose English is quite good, the atmosphere is relaxed.

Chapter 22

Four weeks in Ahvaz is just about as much as we can take. We say goodbye to the cockroaches, which by now are friendly and very tame, and after a four hour train ride to the port we board the ship 'Rohna'. The formidable sight of two large guns, several machine guns and an abundance of lifeboats vividly reminds us of war. Soon we will be entering the war zone. The ship is old and in a dilapidated state. Our quarters are below deck. Heat, lack of air and the smell of cooking from the adjoining dirty kitchen is to accompany us for the six days of our voyage through the Persian Gulf to Karachi in India. The cabins on the decks above water level are occupied by First Aid rooms, a mini hospital and the people who are in charge of the transport. Our large hall, which holds about two hundred people, is divided into two halves. One half is taken over by wooden tables and benches – our dining room. The other half is filled with straw mattresses and small pillows – our bedroom. As soon as we put our luggage down we are assembled on deck, given life jackets and instructed how to put them on and told never to be without them. We are not allowed to go out on deck after nightfall. Ala confesses to me that she is very worried about her diary. "If, in an emergency, we have to jump into the sea and the boat sinks, my diary will be ruined for ever!" she says. My assurance that if we survive this voyage I shall be able to recollect all our experiences so she can write them down all over again doesn't appeal to her.

From the very first day we have special drills lasting half an hour. We are taught what to do and how to behave in case we have to abandon ship. I can just imagine the confusion among so many women and children. I can't bear to think about it and have a feeling that our Captain, instead of taking us to Karachi, would rather be on a warship in the midst of battle.

The rickety old ship sails surprisingly quietly and smoothly through the Persian Gulf. The views are magnificent. The shores overgrown by lush, green vegetation look very peaceful. Tall coconut trees sway gently in the breeze and the bluish-green sea is calm. Leaning against the boat's railings I absorb the tranquility of our surroundings. The life-jacket, which I have with me, annoys me and is troublesome. Several machine-guns on the upper deck seem very unnecessary.

It is lunch time. Soon mother or Ala will be looking for me. I don't want to go down below deck. I am not hungry. The English breakfast we had, our very first one, will last me till dinner time or even until the next day. I wonder why the English eat so much first thing in the morning. A greasy, fried sausage and eggs seem a very unlikely menu for breakfast, but that's what the English eat, we are told.

The very hot, yet invigorating fresh sea air is so different from the sweltering, almost choking atmosphere of our bedroom-cum-dining hall, where rats and cockroaches breed. Every evening before I settle down to sleep I thoroughly examine my straw mattress; I have a fear that one day I might find a rat's nest in my bed. Some people say that it is a good sign to see so many rats about, as there is a widespread belief that rats can sense approaching danger well ahead of a disaster actually happening and they leave the ship before it sails. I am sure it is a lot of silly talk.

For the last couple of days the ship has been sailing through the Arabian sea. We are now near land and are entering the port of Karachi in India, our last stop before we sail for East Africa. Our camp is situated fifteen kilometres from the town. The location is dreadful. The large tents are bunched together in a sandy, flat desert, and the whole camp is surrounded by wire fencing. The blazing sun is merciless and the tents are like furnaces inside. They are furnished with wooden beds, a luxury we didn't have in other camps, but the problem is how to sleep on them. Every joint of their wooden frames and the thick criss-cross ropes which form their base are filled with bed bugs. Amazingly quickly they get to know about our presence and start to come out of their hiding places, hungry for our blood. Within the first half an hour Ala and I counted and killed fifty of them. I have so many itchy bites all over my body that another few hundred bed bug bites won't make much difference. However, mother is disgusted with the situation. "These beds should have been burned long ago, and not be given to us to sleep on. The best solution is to stack them up in one corner of the tent and sleep on the sandy ground", mother says. The canteen set up in one of the tents is dirty and the food is only just bearable.

In Karachi, more noticeably than in any other port of call, the English soldiers running the camps are unfriendly. They don't try to hide the fact that our presence here is an extra and unnecessary nuisance. They get impatient when, in spite of trying hard, we don't understand what they are saying to us. Their unjustified superior manner is very tiresome.

Every time we are in the canteen the same young soldier comes up to our table with a packet of English biscuits. Every time mother, who is very annoyed with their general behaviour, refuses. And every time, Ala who knows five sentences in English says: "We no speak English". He smiles and walks away.

We stay in this devilish camp for six long days and five sleepless nights. Laughing, hungry hyenas keep us awake most nights. Via Karachi, transports of Poles, mainly Polish orphans, sail to Bombay, Mexico and New Zealand. We are going to Uganda in East Africa.

Chapter 23

The ship 'California' is taking us across the Indian Ocean to Mombasa. It is a much bigger ship than the previous one and, though her shell is freshly painted, the inside is very dirty and decrepit. I have a feeling that after this voyage her next destination will be the scrap-yard. Our quarters, as on 'Rohna', are below deck. Our duties, apart from washing up after meals, are to scrub sticky tables and floors. These daily chores are very necessary and understandable on a boat with several hundred people crammed into all the places which were not originally intended for passengers. The only snag is the heat and the lack of air; the rusty old ventilators below deck don't work.

The readiness and abundance of guns, machine-guns and lifeboats fills me with dread. This time the possibility of meeting Japanese and German submarines is very real. The convoy of warships which appear on the horizon as soon as we set sail onto the open sea emphasises the situation. The Captain and the crew are Scottish. The majority of the sailors are young men; they don't look more than seventeen or eighteen years old. The discipline is very rigorous and the young, almost childish, boys are very much afraid of their stern, fierce-looking Captain. They are not allowed to talk to us, which is just as well because their Scottish accent is extremely baffling. The sailors, in spite of being watched closely and seemingly afraid to step out of line, are very generous toward the children. Whenever they have the opportunity and the Captain or the officers are not around, they share their rations of sweets and fruit with them. The officers have much more freedom; they walk about the decks smiling discreetly at the pretty girls. One day, the ever-vigilant Captain catches sight of an officer engaged in a friendly conversation with a young woman. He walks past the couple and his ragged grim face becomes even grimmer, yet he says nothing. However, for the next three days the unlucky young man is nowhere to be seen. "I am told he is in detention", Ala says. "One would think we all had the plague!"

Every morning at 10.00 a.m. sharp, we go through the emergency drill. As we all know very well that these drills are only trial exercises, we behave sluggishly and without real urgency, to the great displeasure of the Captain. One day about half way to Mombasa, in the middle of a quiet and leisurely afternoon, the majority of us are out on the deck enjoying the hot, fresh sea air. We are watching with interest a school of dolphins swimming by. We are so engrossed in their spectacular high jumps and the sleek movements of their big, silver bodies that the very sudden hooting sounds announcing approaching danger are a most unexpected and shocking interruption. We are told that an enemy ship has been sighted. Without delay the sailors, wearing helmets and life-jackets, start to lower the lifeboats, quickly and skilfully. Some take positions by the guns, others try to organise us, making sure that our inseparable life-jackets are correctly worn. Pandemonium breaks out. Women are screaming looking for children, children are crying looking for their mothers. After about twenty minutes of utter confusion, during which the sailors unsuccessfully try to restore some order, we are told through the loudspeakers that this is only an exercise. We draw a sigh of relief. The sailors seeing our stunned faces breaking into smiling relief are so amused that they laugh openly. I think our Captain has finally reached his goal, he has taught us a lesson, because from this day onwards our daily drills are nothing short of perfect.

Soon we are to cross the Equator. Ala and I are standing on the deck watching the vast ocean. I feel very excited and full of anticipation. The sun is beating down and the dark-green sea glistens. "Why are you so fidgety!" Ala asks me, fanning herself with her diary. "If you expect to see a line going through the waters and feel a sudden heat-wave, you're going to be very disappointed. We won't know when we are at the Equator, unless we are told by the sailors." Ala still treats me like a child, I think with annoyance, walking away from her and grateful that no one overhead her silly comment.

Mother surprises me time and again. Today, to our displeasure, she refuses an offer of a cabin for the three of us. The man in charge of the transport knew father before the war and now feels that his family should be travelling in more suitable accommodation. When we asked her why she doesn't accept his very tempting proposition, she simply says that we can't leave our friends with whom we have been travelling since Pahlavi, and a few more days of discomfort won't make much difference.

Through our journey the constant escort of the warships reminds us of war, but I try to ignore their horrid presence and, in spite of daily drills, oppressive heat and the stench below deck, I am sorry that soon we will leave 'California'. The rusty dilapidated ship has brought us safely across the ocean and, though a few times during rough seas she rocked, bounced and creaked, and mother plus a lot of others felt very sick, I have enjoyed every minute of this voyage. When the wind drops, the beautiful Indian Ocean seems very peaceful and yet full of fascinating under-water life. Gregarious dolphins often follow our ship. Only yesterday, the sailors pointed out to us the torpedo-like shapes lurking in the water, the whales. These large, imposing creatures betray their presence while breathing, producing a fountain of water visible a mile or more away. My curiosity is always stirred by the small greenish-brown fish which appear to have tiny wings; they leap out of the water in a glittering cascade, stay in the air for a short while and dive back into the sea. From time to time masses of jelly fish form cloudy patches beneath the surface of the water.

Our ship docks in Mombasa on the 9th of November 1942. Yesterday was my thirteenth birthday. For the following six teenage years of my life my home is to be in the heart of the African jungle. On the decks the sailors are waving and, though I can detect a trace of relief in our Captain's steely eyes as we leave the boat, he is smiling in a friendly manner.

"Goodbye 'California'."

Chapter 24

For several years Africa is to be a refuge for homeless Poles. To its shores ships bring over eighteen thousand people. The camps are scattered over North and South Rhodesia, Tanganyika, Kenya and Uganda – our destination, a beautiful African country by the shores of Lake Victoria.

We board the trains without delay and travel for three days. The train speeds through rolling savannah. Herds of giraffe, antelope, zebra and gazelle graze on the yellow grasslands. I look through the train's window hoping to spot a cheetah hiding in a tree or a lion feasting on its kill. Birds of prey circle lazily in the blue sky. The beauty of this untamed land is irresistible. In our tedious travels we covered several thousand miles, yet never before have I felt such a tingling excitement at seeing a new country. Now, sitting on a hard bench in the train, I have a strange feeling of unreality. Am I reading an adventure story or am I dreaming? Because if I am dreaming I don't want to wake up. Through the partially open window a gust of hot, dusty air blows right into my face and the blazing sun burns my bare arms, but this doesn't bother me; I can sit by this window for hours. I am so mesmerised by what I see and feel that I can hardly concentrate on the lecture being given to us by a Polish doctor. She is trying to acquaint us with the living conditions and the tropical climate awaiting us.

I know what mosquitoes and malaria are, I have heard about amoebic dysentery, but what are jiggers? "Jiggers are very small black fleas living in the soil", the doctor says. "They lay their tiny eggs in human flesh, feet of course are their favourite place. They get under the toe-nails or under the skin around the nails and there they hatch their eggs. If the feet are not inspected daily and the jiggers and their eggs are not removed in time, the toes become inflamed, gangrene sets in and eventually the toes have to be amputated. Soon we will be able to see for ourselves the result of negligence, as a lot of natives are toeless." On this cheerful note, the doctor ends her lecture and moves to the next carriage.

We stop in Nairobi for a couple of hours. Here my first direct meeting with black people is more or less what I had imagined. They look friendly and smile a lot. Their teeth, exposed in a broad grin, are sparkling white but their smooth, shiny skin is much darker than I expected. Some wear long white gowns, but the majority have merely a loincloth and rows of bright beads around their necks. It seems that their only role is to serve the white people. They fetch and carry or just stand around waiting for orders.

A group of English ladies and a native brass band welcome us. Tables arranged on the station platform are laden with egg and tomato sandwiches, little sponge cakes with pink and white icing and tropical fruit – oranges, bananas, pineapple and fruit unknown to us, such as mangoes and papayas. I never thought that there were so many varieties of bananas, my favourite fruit. Some are very large and their tough green skin hides soft, pink and almost juicy pulp. Some are short and chubby with a very strong aroma and paper-thin, yellow skin. The least tasty ones are small, triangular-looking and curved more than the others.

Another stop, at Eldoret, and another friendly welcome. We reach Namasagal after three days travel and board barges on the Victoria Nile. Even though I have had little sleep since we left the 'California' I am not at all tired. The trip on the Nile is a very rejuvenating experience. I can hardly believe my eyes and point constantly at the banks lined with thick reeds of papyrus and bushes with a profusion of everlasting flowers. Fat crocodiles, some twelve feet long, bask lazily in the hot sun; some flip quietly into the river, others watch us with beady eyes. They look sluggish and grossly over fed. They seem harmless, but I know they are dangerous. Ala continually moans that no one has a camera. "Photographs would be a splendid supplement to my diary", she says. Ala is right. What a pity we can't immortalise what we have seen and what we are seeing now; words are not enough to describe it. The endless sun-scorched Kazakhstan steppes, Razin buried under the snow in the grip of the fierce Russian winter, Iran, India, the sea voyage and now beautiful East Africa.

After thirty-six hours on the barges we arrive in a port on the Nile, Messinga. Here lorries are waiting for us. At first the dirt track road cuts through an open grassland. A herd of gloomy-looking buffalo watches us warily. A giraffe nibbles on tender young leaves of a thorny acacia tree. The tiny villages scattered around are homes of the Masai tribe. Their small, round, straw and mud huts look like giant beehives. I see a young boy sitting outside a hut shaping a pot out of strips of clay. A little further is a banana plantation, further still a lush forest of wild figs, date-palms and mahogany trees. Two hours drive through the Bunyoro forest jungle is the very last leg of our long journey. A humid twilight and dense layers of greenery on both sides of a road that has deteriorated into a mass of holes and ruts looks very mysterious. An extraordinary variety of howls, screams and trills echo down from the canopy of the jungle, and fill me with agitation. The roots covered in moss and dangling lianas remind me of 'Tarzan' films, which I enjoyed very much a few years ago, back in Poland. I never imagined then that I would one day be in then middle of this dim, twilight world.

The jungle vibrates with life. Small mischievous-looking monkeys perform acrobatic acts, leaping effortlessly from tree to tree; some swing on the twisted lianas or just sit amongst the branches looking at us with interest. A family of chimpanzees, up in a tree, produces such an outcry of delight from all of us that our African driver stops the lorry to let us have a better look at their clever, almost human faces. Noisy parrots clamber among the leaves, slender dragon-flies flutter their large transparent wings and clouds of tiny insects fill the air with a continuous buzz. Brilliantly coloured butterflies form large patches of pulsating mosaic on the corrugated road in front of us and, as we drive forward, they rise up in a rainbow cloud, only to settle down again a few yards away from the moving lorry.

Mother looks tense. Another mile or two and our travels will end. But where are we driving to? There is no sign of a town or a village. The jungle is just as dense and impregnable and the very bumpy, narrow road is getting even worse. Suddenly the lorry stops. "This is our camp Masindi!" a delegator who met us in Messinga informs us. In front of us lies a small piece of land partially freed from the exuberant vegetation; terrain snatched from the jungle by man. For many weeks before our arrival a couple of hundred natives struggled with nature, hacking with big, broad knives at trees, bushes, tangled roots and two-metre-high elephant grass, until they cleared a space large enough to erect several straw huts. The huts look like enormous rectangular baskets covered by layers of elephant grass and huge banana leaves. Each hut holds eighteen people, and the bunk beds inside it are made from bamboo sticks.

The torrential tropical rain which comes soon after our arrival demonstrates that the roofs of the huts are not waterproof. We and our belongings are completely drenched. Thank goodness it is the middle of November and very soon the rainy season will be over.

Mother tries very hard to appear calm and unconcerned, yet I know she is very worried. She even jokes that we won't need to bother with dresses as a loin cloth will be a most suitable outfit in these primitive surroundings. Some women become quite hysterical. "We will be eaten alive by wild beasts", they cry. The thick and tangled undergrowth of the forest is only a few feet away from the huts and is alive with tropical snakes and spiders. They seem to ignore the invasion of their territory by humans. Amazingly, as I later recalled, during our six-year stay in the jungle no one was bitten by a poisonous snake. Very often during my rambling walks, shiny, zig-zaggy snakes slip from under my feet, but they never try to attack me. One day to my horror I find a beautifully marked snake coiled snugly under my mattress. Ala and I carry the bed out of the hut and with a long stick, and my heart in my throat, I coaxed it out. 'Wild beasts', those who would like to eat us, to my great disappointment keep away from the camp. A visit from a tiger or a lion in the middle of a dark and humid night would make a lovely and very exciting story. A variety of agile small monkeys are our only, but frequent, visitors. They look at us appealingly and, whenever they have a chance, they steal a banana. With anticipation I wait for maybe a gorilla, but they too prefer the undisturbed depth of the jungle.

Within a week of our arrival we become acquainted with

ant-eaters. The very first one, a giant pangolin, arouses great excitement and fear. Its armoured body is bulky and rounded and looks fearsome, but in fact the ant-eaters are harmless and are only interested in ants and termites, eating them very nimbly. There is no shortage of ants here. Red ants and black ants, tiny, medium and big. Their bites are very painful and itchy. The ant hills and the enormous reddish mud fortresses built by the termites are everywhere. The termites chomp their way through decaying twigs and rotten wood, but they don't just eat wood, they eat paper, leather and cloth too. They tunnel beneath the surface of the soil or cover their tracks and themselves with layers of masticated mud. At night, to save our shoes from being devoured by termites, we hang them on bamboo sticks, protruding from the hut's roof. One day I leaned against our table which stands by the wall and the table collapsed and I with it. During the night unceasingly busy termites munched through the three legs of the table, leaving only a paper-thin layer of mud. Ala hides her diary under a pillow for fear of the greedy termites.

The dry season is upon us and the weather is extremely hot. In the noon-day still, when the sun beats down on us, one can actually see the hot air vibrating. We are issued with tropical helmets made of cork and must not go out without them. The red soil dries up and cracks. The threshing floors in the huts have to be sprinkled with water several times a day to keep down the red, fine dust.

Chapter 25

We have now been in the first transit camp for about six weeks. The new transport is arriving from Mombasa and we are moving to our new accommodation. All around us the natives are working hard. Bit by bit they steal more ground from the jungle. Once the site is cleared they build more huts. The new huts look a little better. They are divided into three rooms, one for each family. The straw walls come up only three-quarters of the way and are covered all over with mud. The thick straw roof seems much more reliable. Eventually three kilometres of the jungle is taken over by 'Refugee Camp Masindi'. The camp consists of six small villages and holds 3,635 people. Every village has its own name, and as this is going to be our home for a very long time, the word 'camp' is erased from our vocabulary. We have had enough of camp life. Now we wait for the end of the war and firmly believe that Masindi is just another stop before we can return to our country. Poles are fighting and dying on all fronts and, as soon as the Germans are conquered, Poland will be free once again.

Within a few months of our arrival in Uganda, all the young boys who were not old enough to join the Polish forces at the time of leaving Russia are now of age; their turn has come. One village is entirely occupied by the orphans and from there, more so than from the other villages, the boys of seventeen and eighteen years old are very keen to go to war. I know some of them quite well and have noticed that from that very day they become very sure of themselves and, to my mind, ridiculously cheerful. I truly don't understand the terrible fascination war holds for them and wonder if their bravado is genuine. The day they go is a day of sadness. Grown-ups talk a lot about the war. Now they are saying that the boys won't be taking part in the fighting. "By the time they are trained and are ready for active service, the war will be over", they say. I hope they are right! Once the boys depart the shortage of young men in the villages is more noticeable than ever. "What a dreary prospect of growing up among women, old men and babies!" I say to Ala one day, very eager to hear her comment. But she is quite unconcerned. "I wish I could get in touch with John. He is probably fighting or he might be dead and I know nothing about it!" Ala says unexpectedly. And I thought she had forgotten John!

We hardly have time to settle down in our straw huts and already the schools are being organised. The prospect of having to sit for hours depresses me. However, I am reluctantly beginning to accept the idea that very soon swotting will start in earnest. Three and a half years have passed since my school days, as I am not taking into account the few last months spent in the proper school back in occupied Lvov. Then the teachers were made to drum into us the detailed history of the Russian Revolution, all the advantages of the communist system, and above all 'the incomparable kindness of Father Stalin'. This, as I now clearly see, was pure propaganda and brainwashing of the children. I have no illusions now. School has started. The fact that we have no accommodation for the school, not enough teachers and no books, doesn't seem to present a problem. All the children of school age are divided into appropriate groups. Every morning we gather in the shade of the tropical trees and start our lessons. The atmosphere is so non-school like that I can hardly concentrate. One day I notice that the rough, tangled tree root on which I am sitting is covered by tiny red ants and they start crawling all over my dress. My distraction from the lecture is so obvious that the teacher reprimands me sternly. I feign to be deeply sorry for interrupting the lesson but I can't stop fidgeting and the teacher sends me out of the 'classroom'. I look around me. Where shall I go? Ant and termite hills and giant elephant grass surrounds me. I decide to stand behind a tree which is just as good as standing outside a classroom door. While standing there I notice a frighteningly large column of red ants emerging from a dense wall of elephant grass. They are marching in a continuous ribbon about ten inches abreast and several inches deep. They are heading straight for the group of children and the teacher sitting on the other side of the tree. Since I am very annoyed and feel undoubtedly unjustly punished, I don't warn them of the approaching danger. However, at the very last minute when the column of ants is almost upon them my nerve breaks and I raise the alarm.

These very primitive classrooms are only a temporary arrangement. The natives cut down more of the jungle and erect more straw huts. They have no windows, but the walls are only about one metre high and it is nice and bright inside. They are to be our proper school for the years to come. In time we have desks, benches and blackboards. We have primary and secondary school and a school where various trades are taught. Apart from all the usual subjects we have English, French, Latin and music lessons. Only a few are professional teachers, the rest are people who know their subject and are willing to help. Mother teaches Polish in primary school. The situation improves when quite by chance, in the Mission nearest to us, a Polish missionary arrives. He has been in Uganda for several years and as soon as he hears about our considerable difficulties he supplies the school with books, paper, pens, pencils and elementary books for learning English. At the beginning, for each subject, we only have one book per class. The hours after school are spent copying the lessons. In the first year we go through three years of school programme, to make up for lost time. The enforced discipline is good for all of us and Ala and I take our school work very seriously.

Even though some of our self-proclaimed teachers are far from good and we are lacking a lot of the most essential school aids, the school has surprisingly good results. Proof came in 1948 when we eventually arrived in England. Quite a few of our friends, after an intensive crash-course in English, were admitted to colleges and universities to become teachers, solicitors, doctors, architects and a variety of other professions.

The youth club is another great and welcome improvement in our lives that are starved of normality. A gramophone and an old piano transported from Kampala provide entertainment. We gather there to listen to the music or simply for a laugh and a chat. The school dances for senior pupils are the envy of my friend and me; we are supposed to be too young to join them. Every time there is a dance we sit hidden in the bushes outside the Club, watching with jaundiced eye the older girls dancing with each other, as there are not enough boys to go round. The sound of waltzes and tangos in the depth of the jungle, where until now only tom-tom drums sounded, intrigues the natives. They stop in their lazy stride to listen. Amazingly quickly they pick up the tune and hum it. The sounds of tom-tom drums are the means of communication between the natives' villages; they are their bush telephones. Every night, apart from the usual mysterious noises of the jungle, the rhythmical drums beat out their message in the distance. The tropical nights are very different from everything I have experienced until now. The immensely deep dark sky is always cloudless and very lavishly studded with bright stars. The frequency with which the shooting stars dart across the sky rouses my curiosity. I have asked several people why here in Africa one can see so many shooting stars, but no one can give me an answer.

At night throughout the dry season the horizon is red with the glare of fire; the jungle and bushes are burning. Although several kilometres separate us from the fires, their intensity must be very great as the flames are easily visible. At first we feel very uneasy, fearing that the mighty fires will creep slowly towards our villages. The huge, untamable bush fires don't reach us, yet we do have our share of fires starting in the villages. We dread them the first year in Masindi. They usually start as a result of the natives burning the bush and elephant grass around the villages to get rid of snakes, lizards and the masses of tropical insects, including the most frightful big spiders, which invade our huts. During the windy days, those whose homes are next to the bushes implore the natives not to start the fire but their pleas are usually ignored. One exceptionally windy day vividly demonstrates how very real the people's fears are. The dry grass crackles vigorously and burning bits fly in the air; any minute now and they will start falling on top of the straw roofs. The agitated and worried occupants of the huts nearest to the burning bush start to evacuate their belongings. Under these conditions only a miracle can prevent the impending disaster. But the miracle doesn't happen. Before anyone has time to empty their homes, four roofs catch fire and immediately bright orange flames engulf them. They burn with such ferocity that within a very short time they become a heap of smouldering ash. We all run to help. Ala runs first, mother runs after Ala trying to stop her, I run after mother. Thick, curling smoke chokes and stings the eyes, clouds of soot linger in the air. A fifth hut is now in great danger. Long tongues of fire lick bamboo poles which support the roof. People shout and cry. A woman rushes out of the hut with a small child in her arms. Her plaited, full skirt brushes against the burning bamboo pole and catches fire. Mother grabs the child from her, throws it to me like a ball, and pulls the woman down to the ground. Quickly she scrapes dry soil and strews handfuls of it over the burning skirt. Thanks to mother's amazing presence of mind, the woman sustained only very superficial burns. The fight with the fire goes on. The natives with long sticks, clubs and spears beat down the flames to prevent them from spreading further. Their terrified, chanting cries sound like ritual black magic songs. With their bare feet they jump up and down attempting to smother it. Everyone tries to help. The other children and I scoop up handfuls of dusty soil from the road and pour it over the little fires which start to flare up wherever there are dry bits of grass or bamboo sticks, and there are a lot of them. We are afraid that the whole village will burn down. In the midst of this inferno, Ala's friend has her foot pierced accidentally by a native's sharp spear. The blood gushes out and Ala faints.

I am very impressed by Ala's heroic attempt to put out the blazing fire, but still glad she fainted at the first sight of blood and had to be carried away. For a long time afterwards, whenever we see the natives' villages burning, as often happens, she pales and starts to tremble. Until now I thought that fire was fought by water, but not here. The water wells are not finished and to pump out one pail of water is a hard and time-consuming job. The news of the fire spreads quickly but by the time the English officials arrive we have it under control.

For several weeks afterwards we keep a look out, especially at night, and a couple of black policemen patrol the villages. Though the first disaster was the worst, and during the first year other fires started occasionally, we are beginning to get as used to them as to everything else in our lives. The indestructible elephant grass keeps growing, despite constant efforts to burn it down.

Chapter 26

The war goes on and on, long months go by and from time to time our secluded, peaceful world is shattered by news from the front. For some the short chilling sentence, "Killed in action", is a tragic realisation that they will never again see their fathers, husbands or sons. The knowledge of our boys being wounded, missing or killed is for me an eye-opener on how cruel this war is. I am very thankful that our father is much too old to be fighting in the war. He is in Egypt now in an army camp in the desert. His long letters are very interesting. He tells us about the scorpions which creep into his tent at night and he describes in detail the desert life of the bedouins. He has seen the pyramids and the sphinx. I can just imagine his interest and excitement while he visits these wonders of the world. He told me once about the Pharaohs and the priests; now he is in their domain himself. In his last letter he says that he will probably be able to join us soon in Uganda for a two-year leave from the army. Although I am bursting with happiness and excitement at the prospect of seeing father again, I control myself, as only recently our neighbour was notified by the War Office that her husband and eighteen-year-old son were killed in action. The conviction is growing in me that God's hand protects us and once again I tell myself how very lucky we are.

The tropical climate doesn't suit mother. She is one of the first to get amoebic dysentery. The three Polish doctors have a supply of essential drugs and do whatever they can to help the people. At the beginning malaria prevails. Mosquito nets are compulsory. They have to be tucked well under the mattress to prevent the little nasty insects from getting inside. We are advised not to go near the damp, humid woods after sunset, as they are a breeding ground for mosquitos. Despite all the precautions, everyone has an attack of malaria, not once but several times. I look upon my first attack of malaria with a certain affection, as malaria saved me from making a fool of myself during a maths lesson. I detest maths and, although I previously knew that I would be asked to solve a complicated mathematical problem in front of the whole class, I didn't prepare myself. At the very beginning of the lesson, the teacher asks me to come up to the blackboard. I get up from behind my desk and suddenly feel my whole body trembling. "Stop shaking like a leaf, the teacher is not going to eat you!" my friend whispers. I try to control the tremor, but I don't succeed. Shivering violently I reach the blackboard. Several numbers and letters written on it look like a jig-saw puzzle. I haven't got a clue where to start. My teeth chatter and the skin on my arms is like goose-flesh. I am surprised that my anxiety and fear is so noticeable. A piece of chalk which I try to hold in my trembling hand falls to the floor. The teacher looks at me for a while and then says: "Barbara, you should be in bed, not in front of the blackboard, you have got malaria!" Phew, what a relief!

I am cursed with tropical ulcers on both my legs. The very deep, weeping sores don't heal. The doctors try every possible ointment, but nothing seems to help. For daily dressings I, and others who have tropical ulcers, visit a medical centre which is set up in one of the huts for dressings. The months go by, the Medical Centre changes into a small hospital but I still have the ulcers and they are not improving. I am getting very concerned about the look of my legs. Not only are they much fatter than Ala's, but now they are going to have horrible scars all over them, if ever they heal. One day, instead of the usual smelly ointment, the nurse puts thick slices of fresh tomato over the ulcers. I am so fed up with the bandages which cover both my legs from the knees downward that I don't care any longer. "You must be short of ointment," I comment. To my delight after a few days of the tomato treatment, the ulcers begin to shrink and the deep holes in my calves slowly start to fill out with new flesh. I marvel at the astonishing healing powers the tomatoes possess.

The dressing of inflamed, pussy toes caused by nasty jiggers is the main job load of the nurses. Neither mother, Ala nor I need their attention. Every night before we go to bed, with a sharp point of a needle, we remove the tiny pests before they have a chance to settle down and lay their eggs. Mother has a couple of elderly 'patients' who come regularly to have their feet inspected, as this operation requires very sharp eyesight and a steady hand.

Our small hospital is built from rich, red mahogany, the most easily obtainable wood. It has three wards with forty beds on each ward. Thanks to our doctors who believe that prevention is better than cure, many of the beds are empty. On one occasion I occupied a hospital bed for three days. Under the roof of our straw hut we have a massive cone-shaped mud nest, which is a busy swarming place for huge, jet-black African wasps. They always appear extremely laborious, flying in and out of the hut. Although they bother us and are very obnoxious, no one dares get rid of the nest. Their malicious stings can be excruciatingly painful and even dangerous. One day one of them stings my back. Within minutes my whole body swells up, my puffed eyelids begin to close. Though tears stream down my face I am completely dumb. With frightening speed my tongue and the inside of my throat swell up as well. I feel that I am choking. I run to the hospital as fast as my bloated legs can carry me. I can't utter a word, but a nurse, seeing that I am twice my usual size, quickly leads me to see a doctor. After several injections I return to normal, but have to stay in hospital for three days.

Unfortunately mother spends a lot of time in the hospital, troubled by amoebic dysentery and severe attacks of malaria. I hate it when mother is away, not only because I miss her very much, but also because Ala bosses me around. The other day she noticed that my friend does my maths homework for me while I write an essay for her. Now she threatens to disclose our secret pact. Like mother she fusses if, during the day, I go out without my cork helmet on, and is very much against our lovely grey cat sleeping on my bed. I don't know how the very first cat appeared in the camp but I know that now we have several hundred of them roaming around and they keep on multiplying. The majority of them are homeless, wild and very neglected. During one of mother's stays in the hospital, our cat gives birth to a litter of six adorable kittens. Very thrilled, we tell mother about the happy event but mother doesn't share our excitement. "Regretfully, you have to drown them now, while they are only a couple of hours old", mother says from her hospital bed, looking at Ala and expecting her to be the executioner. I know very well that Ala is not going to be a party to this mass murder. I can see her stiffen but she says nothing. At home she looks with pity at the bundle of kittens and categorically pronounces that she is not going to do it. Years have passed since that time but I still cringe at the thought of that dreadful day as I was the one who had to drown the little helpless creatures in the deep hole in the outside shed which served as our toilet.

Chapter 27

Masindi is a green paradise and, as it is situated between two large lakes, Lake Albert and Lake Kioga, the vegetation is lush and exuberant. Every hut in the village is surrounded by a garden. Exotic flowers, banana trees, spiky pineapples, potatoes, tomatoes, sweetcorn and enormous sunflowers grow vigorously, constantly battling with the invading strong elephant grass, which would very quickly engulf every village if it wasn't for our endless endeavours to burn it or cut it down.

In our back garden we have a small enclosure where we keep a hen, a cockerel and now five beautiful chicks. The pair are small and very ordinary looking, but clever and with strong parental instincts. Every time before a tropical storm breaks out, the hen senses the imminent change in the weather and leads her five chicks into our hut to protect them from the torrential rain. The father cockerel wins fights with snakes who creep towards the enclosure where the chicks are. The end of this loving family is very sad. The day comes when the dedicated parents can't save the chicks or themselves from the voracious power of the red ants. The ants not only eat the whole chicken family, but they almost ate Ala.

One night Ala's hysterical screams wake the whole household. We jump out of our beds. Mother lights a paraffin lamp and what we see fills us with horror. A massive unbroken column of red ants is marching down from the garden and through our hut. Ala's bed is in their path. The mosquito net doesn't divert or stop them in their track; they get inside through the tiny holes and take over the bed. Ala looks as if she is having convulsions. She rips off her night-dress and shakes her head violently; her hair is full of ants. She is panic-stricken. Once Ala is freed of the ants and calms down a little, we stand back and watch. It is best not to disburb the ants. It takes them over an hour to pass through our hut, leaving behind Ala's body dotted with numerous red bumps, her nerves shattered for the rest of the night, and a heap of clean chicken bones.

My friend has two small silvery grey monkeys. Their frequent visits are a result of greed. Ground peanuts and bananas are their favourite diet and then, as soon as they get their ration, they disappear into the jungle. These fleeting visits annoy and upset my friend. "If they only come to satisfy their appetite, I don't want to see them again!" she says to me. "Next time they are not going to be fed!" In a couple of days the cheeky pair appears at the doorstep. My friend, true to her promise, ignores them and hides all the food. For the best part of the day they follow her around, pulling at her dress. However, seeing that their persistency has no result, they try a different approach. Snuggled closely together, they sit in a corner of the room crying and, at the same time, watching her every move. Needless to say, my friend soon gives in to their crafty game and offers them a banana feast. Now she wishes that she had never encouraged them from the beginning. The whole house is in an uproar. They have taken it over. Most nights they sleep on her bed or they swing on the mosquito net, reducing it to shreds. They tear her books and hide her shoes. She is often late for school and she blames it on the two little horrors. I have stopped going to see her as my long plaits are one more toy for them to play with.

Watching my friend's life being ruined by these monkeys, I am rapidly changing my mind about having a monkey as a pet. I apply all my skills to taming a chameleon. In our garden we have quite a few of them and they don't seem to be afraid of people. At first I was very wary, not realising that they are only lizards. It took me a long time to gather all my courage to pick one up. I am fascinated by their ability to change colour to match their background but, at the same time, I am very disappointed that they don't become blue, yellow or mauve as I previously thought. They only change into all shades of green, brown or black. The strangest thing to see is how each of the chameleon's eyes moves independently of the other one. Although I work hard, I don't think the chameleons like being domesticated.

Chapter 28

Father has arrived. He has been released from the army for two years. The vision of his sunken, yellow cheeks, protruding ribs and grossly swollen legs, which haunted me since Pahlavi, has vanished without a trace. He looks well now and is full of jokes and interesting stories. I am very happy and now, as our family is complete again, I don't care how long we are going to stay here. From Egypt he brought me a gold ring with three turquoise stones and he says that the azure gems are the colour of my eyes.

Within a couple of weeks of his arrival father starts teaching history, his favourite subject, at the secondary school. As he has never taught before he finds his new profession a challenge which he enjoys. Apart from teaching, he is responsible for law and order in the camp. Although this mini police assignment bears no resemblance to his pre-war position, he seems to be very content. I think father has changed. His ability to adapt to the prevailing conditions and his strong desire to make every single day worthwhile is astonishing. He never complains and once said that from the moment he left Russia each day is a gift to be valued and fully used. I am often tempted to ask father what happened in those prison camps but I can never summon up enough courage and he never talks about it. Our frequent moans, that we only have a couple of old dresses to wear and our only footwear is plimsolls, meet with his displeasure. "Have you already forgotten about the time spent in Russia, and the friends who are still there?" father says one day. "Cast your mind back and you will soon realise how very minor your complaints are!" I have not forgotten and I know father is right but I yearn for a pair of leather shoes. If only I could get rid of my grubby plimsolls which make my feet hot and itchy. Unfortunately they are the only obtainable footwear in the camp. Every morning I cover them thickly with wet chalk to make them white, yet before I even reach school, the chalk dries and crumbles away. Thank goodness for mother's ingenuity. She bought two large, white linen sheets in a little Asian shop a few miles away and made two dresses, one for Ala and one for me. The red and black narrow ribbon tape, which she also bought at the shop, she sews criss-cross fashion on the front of the bodices. I am delighted with the final result but Ala is not too happy because the dresses are almost identical. "I hope you are not going to wear your dress on the same day that I do", Ala cautions me. Her very unreasonable demand compels me to trick her every time I want to wear the dress. Before day breaks, when Ala is still fast asleep, I sneak out of bed, put on the dress and go back under the covers pretending to be asleep, waiting for her to wake up. As soon as I see her stir, I emerge slowly from under my mosquito net. Since I am already dressed, Ala has no alternative but to choose another dress from her wardrobe of three outfits.

Our secondary school is preparing a stage play and Ala is taking part. I can't wait for the day when the whole thing will be over with and the fuss dies down, as Ala is a bundle of nerves and very difficult to live with. The half dozen words she has to say in the play don't give her the right to make my life a misery. Making faces in front of a mirror, she continually repeats the words and I am to judge if she is making the desired impression. What really worries her is not what she has to say but how she will look. She is supposed to be dressed in a gown which looks like a crinoline; easier said than done. Mother scans all the neighbouring little Asian shops for suitable material but to no avail. Time is short; two more days left before the big night. Ala is on the verge of tears and mother, dear mother, suddenly jumps up from her chair and tears off the mosquito net which is hanging over the bed. "This is just what is needed! Why didn't I think of this before?" she exclaims. She gets to work straight away; cutting, pinning, sewing, a frill here, a bow there. To make the skirt very full, so it resembles a crinoline, she sacrifices yet another mosquito net. "We shall replace them next week", she says with a wicked smile. The play is a great success and Ala looks stunning.

Father's position as 'The Chief of Police' and 'lecturer' promotes us to the elite of the camp. We are moving to another straw hut which, together with about a dozen other identical huts, forms a street at the foot of a small mountain, only a short distance away. A dusty, sloping verge, overgrown in places by wild grass, separates the street from the rest of the villages. I am very pleased with the move for the simple reason that at last we are going to have the whole hut all to ourselves. The other huts on this street are occupied by the commandant of the camp and his family, the people who work in administration, our three doctors, a few teachers and the priests. Once some witty person jokingly referred to our street as "The street of Masters" and the name has stuck. I am not very sure if I like the name because since we moved to our new home I think I can detect a slight animosity amongst some of my so-called friends. Ala says that, as usual, I am imagining things.

We now have a 'boy'; his name is Farasico. He is a black youth of about twenty who lives in a nearby village. He wears a long, loose shirt whose dazzling whiteness emphasises his jet black, shiny skin and the symmetrical facial scars are not only ornaments but also distinguish him from members of other tribes. He comes to us every morning and his duty is 'to serve' us. From the very first day, Farasico, Ala and I become very good friends. But Farasico knows he has to keep his distance; we, the white race, are the masters and, though we smile at him and try to talk to him, he never enters the hut without permission. Most of the day he sits in the shade of the banana tree, muttering in a low voice. At first we thought that he is praying to one of his many gods but we later learned that he is a Christian and, like us, worships only one God and the muttering is not a prayer but a jungle song. Some days he brings with him a musical instrument which looks like a miniature harp. Resting it on his crossed legs he touches the strings very gently with his long and slender fingers and hums. He has a very good ear for music and soon is able to play the simple melodies we sing to him. It is very difficult to communicate with Farasico. His language is Swahili, ours is Polish. The English language is a very rickety bridge between us. He knows three words: Master, Madam and baby. He calls us 'baby'. We know a little more but he doesn't understand us. Unexpectedly quickly Farasico learns Polish words and even the long and difficult ones he pronounces perfectly. His ability for learning stimulates us into spending more time teaching him and, at the end of our stay in East Africa, Farasico is able to conduct a simple conversation in Polish and in English. To show him that we are willing to learn his language, I buy a small book of phrases in Swahili. My first attempt to talk to him in his native tongue meets with his delight and uncontrollable laughter.

Although Farasico's mind is quick, his young body is slow. His leisurely walk and every movement of his strong arms are very unhurried. For him the day is as long as he wishes to make it. He fetches fresh water and tends to our small garden. In the garden there is very little for him to do because father is a keen gardener and in his spare time likes to dig the soil or weed the flower beds. The only thing we make sure Farasico does regularly is to cut down the elephant grass, which, if neglected, would soon overgrow the garden and our hut. He is afraid of large insects and snakes and is the first one to run away with a shriek. My friendship with chameleons astounds him. One morning he brings with him his girlfriend, whom he calls 'Madam', and asks me to demonstrate to her my immense bravery by handling or stroking them. The affection which I show towards the animals is beyond his comprehension.

Our hut has a small verandah and its straw roof provides shade for homeless mongrel dogs. They wander around the villages looking for food. Sometimes there are five or six of them sprawled across the verandah's floor. They all look alike and are very skinny. I feed them regularly and, though mother told me not to touch them, I try to remove the shiny ticks, bulging with blood, which protrude from the dogs' brown matted fur. Whenever Farasico sees me performing this minor surgery, he closes his eyes, waves his arms frantically and repeats several times: "No baby, no!".

There are days when Farasico is not in his usual happy mood. On these days a narrow string is tied tightly across his forehead and his stride is even slower, so we know he has a headache and the cause of his suffering is the bad behaviour of one of his many girlfriends. Our water supply then has to be rationed; two buckets in the morning and two at night is as much as Farasico can manage. The rest of the day he squats in the shade holding his head in his hands, muttering loudly: "Madam no good, Farasico no good, baby no good!" "Even we are mentioned in his monotonous groans!" Ala says crossly one day, and, testing his obedience, she points at the two empty buckets, trying to persuade him to get more water as she would like to take a bath. I watch with great curiosity and soon see Ala picking up the empty buckets. Our 'boy' has won once again. I am afraid we have spoiled Farasico, for whoever inherits the 'boy' once we leave Africa will have a hard nut to crack. He regards himself far superior to the rest of the young native men who work around the villages, digging the soil or cutting the grass. Whenever they stop for a chat with Farasico he seems to ignore them. They look like beggars and are practically naked. What once was a shirt is a shirt no more. Dirty, torn pockets held by the seams dangle loosely around their lanky bodies, and remains of shorts serve as dirty loin cloths. Into the pockets they put their earned money, 3d for a day's work. Farasico, with his shiny, round cheeks and in his long white shirt, looks like a picture of health and prosperity.

Chapter 29

In recent weeks, on my way back from school, I stop by a small enclosure to look at and admire a family of pigs. In one of the villages an elderly lonely man, once a very successful farmer and the owner of livestock, keeps a couple of pigs. At first he wanted a cow but sleeping sickness caused by the tsetse fly kills cattle in Uganda, so he had to settle for pigs. The man went to a lot of trouble to accomplish his dream and now looks after his pigs with dedication. Two weeks ago his sow produced a litter of four pudgy piglets. He is very happy with his pigs and often says that this little family reminds him of his farm in Poland. When he is in a nostalgic mood, I hear about his cows, horses and pigs which he left behind. He always refers to them by name. He never talks about his wife and three children who died in Russia, only about a month before our release.

Today, like many times since the piglets were born, I stop by the enclosure, noticing with surprise that instead of four, only three piglets are running around and the man, in a state of shock, tells me that someone has stolen one of his young pigs. As soon as I get home I tell father about the crime but father already knows and an investigation has started. During the next few days extensive inquiries, not only in our villages, but also in the nearby villages of the natives, yield no results. Within a couple of months all four pigs vanish without a trace. The mystery baffles father. He is irritable; his policeman's pride has been wounded. He is beginning to apply Sherlock Holmes's methods. He is sniffing the air just in case, from some direction, an aroma of roast pork reaches his nostrils, but no pigs dead or alive.

After about three months and the disappearance of all six pigs, the mystery unravels. A large python, almost thirty feet long, is spotted snugly coiled in one of the gardens. The woman who finds the snake amongst her flower beds raises the alarm with hysterical petrified screams. The news spreads quickly and everyone runs to see the monster. Only the English Commandant of the camp possesses a firearm, therefore someone races to him with the urgent message. We stand around a safe distance away gaping, almost hypnotised, but the grossly overfed python appears to be asleep; he is digesting his prey, basking in the hot sun. After about twenty minutes, which for all of us seems like eternity, the Englishman arrives and, aiming at the snake's head, kills it with a single shot. I am relieved to see that the villain's last victim, crushed and partly digested, is still inside its huge body, otherwise I fear father would be unbearable to live with.

We have two priests but no church. Sunday and daily services are held in the open air. A small altar erected in the shade of a big tree and a few wooden benches for elderly people is our place of worship. We are beginning to feel that the time has come to build a proper church. Therefore a church committee is formed. After a lot of discussions, arguments and pressure from the priests, the main bulk of financial aid is finally secured. The remainder of the money comes from our contributions. We give as much as we can afford. Plans are made and the location decided. On the day when the first foundations are to be laid, the priests bless the site. The people who are gathered around form a long line and ceremoniously start passing the first bricks to the workers, as the actual work of building the church is done by the native bricklayers and labourers. After many months the church is finished and the final result is very pleasing. It looks so solid that I begin to wonder if we are ever meant to leave Masindi. It is the only building made of brick and it is the pride and joy of our small community. It has a spacious nave, a big altar, a central aisle and rows of pews. Several winding cement steps lead to the choir. Every Sunday a small, second-hand organ is played by our music teacher. The teacher is also the leader of the choir formed from the pupils of the secondary school. Although my voice is very insignificant and music sheets confuse me, I am one of its proud members. On the day the music teacher selects his singers my friend Irka, whose voice is exceptionally melodious and clear, stands behind me and, while I am only miming, she sings a scale, modifying her voice so it doesn't sound too good but still much better than mine. Thanks to the teacher's advanced age and failing sight, the deceit has not been noticed. The choir is very good and our efforts are greatly admired. I think I am the only member whose voice is not up to standard.

In Masindi, like in all the other Refugee Camps in Africa, the Boy Scout and Girl Guide movements flourish. There is hardly a young person in the villages who is not a boy scout, girl guide, brownie or cub. The organisation strengthens friendships and engrains in our young hearts our love of God and our country. I greatly enjoy our frequent meetings in the depths of the humid jungle. The eery twilight and calmness of the huge trees that reach the sky gives me an undescribable thrill. To me the jungle is like a different world and people are unwelcome intruders. I tend to whisper whenever I am in the jungle.

During our meetings we look for a clearing and there we sit in a circle on the damp, twisted roots and branches and listen to our leader, who, I must admit, prepares herself well for the meetings. Her instructive stories are usually interesting and luckily not too long or too moralistic. After the story we have a discussion which we try to keep as short as possible. Once the solemn part of the meeting is over, we do what we like. We swing on the long lianas or try our skills at constructing a very wobbly bridge over a wide and deep ditch, using branches, lianas and thick rope, and then daringly walking across it. We pick leaves of tropical plants for nature studies or carefully record in our notebooks all the varieties of butterflies we have seen in the day. As I am quite good at drawing, I make quick sketches of the most unusual ones. On the way back to the villages, marching in a straight column, we sing as loud as we possibly can. Sometimes we go camping. A carefully chosen location is usually a couple of miles away from the villages. There our abilities are tested. We erect tents, make fires, cook and in general are closely watched for tidiness, punctuality, obedience and a lot of other little, unimportant things which are supposed to make up our characters. I am never very keen to go camping but since one of my best friends is a very dedicated girl guide I feel obliged to keep her company. The only activity I really like are the nightly bonfires. A brigade of boy scouts, whom we customarily invite, makes the gathering around the fire that much more enjoyable. In the stillness of the tropical night our songs echo around us and the blazing fire lights up our young faces, creating an atmosphere of lasting comradeship.

Very enjoyable, but unfortunately not too frequent, are the day excursions to Port Butiaba on the shores of Lake Albert. We go there in a bus or a large lorry supplied by the English. Butiaba is several miles away from camp and to go there we have to drive through the jungle. No matter how many times I have an opportunity to be in its depth, each time I see and feel it differently. There are the occasions when the jungle's strange motionless and incredible range of shades of green gives an impression of theatrical decorations and I feel like an actress on a huge stage.

After the jungle comes the sleepy landscape of savannah with its characteristic acacia trees and, in moister places, large balls of bright red or violet flowers. These balls of flowers are very curious. They appear to be growing directly from the ground and their branches or leaves are not visible. A little farther on and the scenery changes again. The surface becomes hilly and very rocky. Here acacia trees are much smaller and prickly bushes and strangely-shaped cacti are the dominating features. Suddenly the narrow dusty road bends sharply and the beautiful lengendary Lake Albert appears in front of us. It spreads majestically in a wide valley and its distant shores are lost in mist.

Although many people visited Butiaba before us, and now I am in a group of twenty, I feel like Robinson Crusoe on a desert island. The tall palm trees and hot silver sand, seemingly untouched by human foot, adds to the sensation. We are told that it is quite safe to swim in the lake. Crocodiles, though very occasionally seen here, prefer to congregate at the outflow of the river Nile. We come home late in the evening with large bunches of wild exotic flowers.

Chapter 30

Ala and I are very excited. Our parents have decided that we should see the Murchison Falls. The very seldom organised trips are an extravagant expenditure not everyone can afford. In our circumstances 40 shillings per person is a lot of money. However, father is very eager for us to go. "It would be unforgivable not to see these wonders of nature while we are here, so very near to them." Mother, while agreeing with father, is a little anxious because of the lions, cheetahs, snakes, crocodiles; the list is endless. All these dangers worry her unceasingly. She tries hard not to sound too concerned as an opportunity such as this should not be missed.

On the day of the expedition Ala and I are ready well before time. Our parents are just as excited as we are. Before we leave father turns to me saying: "Barbara, I want to know all about the trip. Keep your eyes wide open." I feel sorry and somewhat guilty that they are not coming with us, especially father as he would love every minute of it. The expedition to the Murchison Falls consists of a guide, six pupils from our secondary school, including Ala and myself, two teachers and several natives in tropical dress and red fezzes, our porters and guards. The rifles slung across their shoulders prove that mother's fears are not unfounded. Once we leave the jungle the long drive through the African grassland is as interesting as usual. We see elephants under a flight of white birds, I think a variety of heron. We see densely bunched wildebeests, continuously on the move searching for new grazing land, rhinos still and powerful and handsome gazelles and antelopes, leaping in different directions, obviously alarmed by our approaching lorry. After several hours we arrive at the water's edge. A small boat which is to take us as near as possible to the Murchison Falls is waiting for us.

The day is nearing its end. The water which only a few moments ago glittered and twinkled with reflecting lights suddenly grows a dull, dark green and blends with the surroundings. The night is pitch black. We are spending the night on the boat. For a long time I feel restless and agitated and only the continuous croak of frogs finally lulls me to sleep. We are up very early to see the sun rise. I am spellbound by the sheer beauty of nature. The boat advances slowly, breaking large islands of multi-coloured water lilies with her bow. The Nile is narrow at this point and its banks, densely overgrown by bushes and papyrus, are only a few yards away from us, bristling with huge fat crocodiles. Farther down the river herds of hippos snort and loll in the water. One of them bellows loudly, exposing his teeth and orange throat. I am a little uneasy and wonder where we shall find a space free of crocodiles so we can land without risk of being eaten for breakfast. Happily our crew has made this trip many times before and soon we stop and reach the shore safely. About two miles separate us now from the waterfalls.

We climb wet cliffs in single file and the guards, rifles at the ready, position themselves in front and behind us. Here lions and cheetahs are known to hide amongst the rocks and thorny bushes, waiting for their prey. I have an aspiration to see a lion; not a caged, sleepy one, of which I have seen many in zoos, but a free, powerful animal, roaming the African bushland. Yet an encounter with a hippo which unexpectedly crosses my path rapidly changes my mind. Before I realise that a bulky body rambling in the nearby bushes belongs to a vegetarian hippo, my heart misses a beat. The nervous reaction of one of the guards, who at that time is standing by me, dispels my faith in all of them.

I am later told that hippos, though peace-loving creatures, would trample over anyone or anything met in their tracks. The narrow path that winds uphill is covered by mica, a mineral found in granite. The small, silver scales glitter intensely in the bright sunlight. I am totally unprepared for their magical beauty. The glare and twinkling of mica makes me almost giddy. The road to Heaven must look like this. The thunderous roar of rushing water, a transparent cloud of mist and a brightly coloured rainbow which joins two silver banks like an arch of triumph, proclaims the closeness of Murchison

Falls. Another few steps and our aim is achieved. The river narrows and drops four hundred feet in a series of three cascades to the level of Lake Albert.

On the way back, sitting silently on the boat's deck, I am deep in thought. I have a dilemma. How on earth am I going to tell father what I have just seen? To say that Murchison Falls are beautiful is very prosaic and simply not enough. I am lost for words. The small scales of mica glitter on my plimsolls; carefully I shake them off onto my handkerchief. They will be my souvenir.

A red dusty road cuts through the villages. One end of the road slopes downward and joins a fairly wide dirt track which leads out of the camp. The other part of the road ascends gently, passing alongside our hospital, youth club, orphanage and a sports field. At one point it curves sharply, crawls for another several hundred yards and abruptly ends at the tangled, dark wall of the jungle. Huge trunks of fallen trees, entwined by lianas and brightly-flowering bindweeds, mark the place where the natives gave up on the enormous task of lengthening the road. I often wonder, if it is ever finished, where this road is going to lead. This unfinished road is our High Street.

Almost every day a brigade of singing boy scouts or girl guides marches on it, raising clouds of red dust with their regular, strong stride. Often a group of natives walks leisurely on its lopsided edge in a long, single line, one behind the other, balancing large bunches of bananas on their heads. They communicate with each other by short humming sounds which don't resemble words of any language. They stop from time to time to sell their goods to the passers-by. Occasionally a big lorry clatters over its bumpy surface delivering to the camp necessary provisions. With nightfall the road changes its character. It becomes an avenue for those who like to go for an evening stroll, or a meeting place for sweethearts. We named it: "Do whatever you like" street. An encounter with a teacher or, God forbid, a priest while walking at dusk, hand-in-hand with a boyfriend, automatically reduces one's esteem in the teacher's or priest's eye. By now we have quite a few romantically linked couples. The boys who not so long ago were only children, too young to be taken into the army are young men. Rivalry among the young female population is very noticeable. The senior, more cunning girls compete very successfully with us juniors to secure a special place in the hearts and minds of the teenage boys, who are usually at least a couple of years younger than the girls. Until now Ala doesn't seem to bother with boys; evidently John is still her heart throb. However, recently a sickly-looking man appeared on Masindi's horizon and already twice I have seen Ala sitting with him in the youth club. At the last week's dance, which habitually my friend and I spy upon, Ala danced with him almost the entire evening. "What do you see in this skinny, meek-looking man?" I ask Ala crossly. "His eyes are bulging and his mousy hair in thin on top. I hope you are not going to parade with him on 'Do whatever you like' street, it would be disgraceful!" I add maliciously. "I'd rather talk to him than to any of those silly, childish boys. He is intelligent and conversation with him is very interesting", Ala says, looking at me, as if to say – mind your own business. However, I think that it is definitely my business and I am giving my undivided attention to Ala's every move. After a few weeks the maddening situation improves and I am able to relax as their friendship is cooling off. Once again John's letters are her main source of happiness.

Some girls from senior classes befriend the young Englishmen who sometimes visit our camp. At first I am convinced that their friendship is only a clever and crafty scheme to learn English the easy way. But soon it becomes apparent that their courtship is genuine. Many married the young men and settled in East Africa.

Chapter 31

At the beginning of 1945, the war which caused such unspeakable terror and misery for millions of people is almost over. The Germans are losing on all fronts and though the Poles fought, suffered and, most of all, hoped for a free country they have lost as well. The Yalta agreement between the three allied leaders has crushed our dreams of ever going back to Poland. The large chunk of East Poland, including my city Lvov, has been annexed by the Soviet Union and the rest of the country is under the control of the Kremlin.

Father's leave from the army is prolonged for another year or so. He is pleased about it, not only because he can be with us, but also he feels that here he can be far more useful. Apart from carrying out his police duties and teaching history, he is also starting to teach Latin in the lower classes. His knowledge of Latin is a blessing. Whenever I am stuck with a specially difficult paragraph to translate he is always willing to help, but often he points out that Latin is now a dead language and we should concentrate on learning English, as most probably the rest of our lives will be spent in England. In the evenings father is preoccupied by his latest hobby, carving. His carving materials are ivory, ebony, mahogany and buffalo horns. Using only his penknife and a piece of glass for smoothing the surfaces he makes small boxes, paper knives, cigarette holders, pipes, crosses and a variety of other little objects. Mother, in spite of being very good at sewing, knitting and embroidery, now attends evening classes for dressmaking. "God only knows what will happen to us in the years to come. I have to improve my sewing skills as it might be the only means of earning money", she says. Her prediction was very accurate. I can still see her in our old Victorian house in London, bent over her large, industrial machine, sewing from early morning till late at night. Father by then was quite old and very hard of hearing and, although his knowledge of English was good, he was unable to find a job.

Meanwhile our cocooned life in Masindi goes on at its usual slow pace. I love our idyllic surroundings and am quite content, particularly now as one of the boys in my class, whom I like very much, shows me a lot of attention. During the lessons his discreet winks and quick glances at me are very pleasing but totally distract my concentration. I am beginning to wonder if the recent bad marks I got for my algebra homework are not entirely his fault.

His name is Tomek. He is not tall, dark and handsome. He is very ordinary looking, is only just about my height and his very blond hair falls carelessly across his forehead in long untidy strands. But his greyish blue eyes, surrounded by almost white long eyelashes, are always laughing and are very attractive. His ability to play any available instrument, especially the accordion, is amazing. He often plays in our youth club and at the boy scouts' and girl guides' bonfire meetings. Although he is shy and unassuming, he plays his accordion with zest and vigour. One day Tomek asks me to go for a walk with him that evening. I am delighted and try hard not to sound too eager. Before I go I plait my long hair with special care and very sparingly apply some oil on my eyebrows and lashes to darken their appearance. To make my plimsolls look more respectable I put an extra layer of wet, white chalk all over them, and am really very thankful that their heel-less style does not make me taller than him.

Ala on the other hand is in a restless mood. Last week she got a long letter from John and since then nothing seems to be right. She confesses to me that she feels as if she is living in limbo. "Our youth is unredeemed. What is going to happen to all of us? Our schooling is hardly adequate. The few books we have we read time and again and when eventually we leave Africa, we won't know how to behave in the civilised world! And look at my teeth!" she exclaims at the end. "We don't even have a decent dentist to look after our teeth which, after two years of starvation in Russia, need constant attention and care!" Poor Ala, she has had a nasty toothache for the last few days and I suppose this accounts for her bad mood. Contrary to Ala's feeling, I look upon this time as a very special phase in my life and I don't feel that the years spent in Uganda have been wasted. But her bitter remarks stir my memories. Many years have passed since that terrifying night when we were practically pulled out of our beds by Russian soliders, many years since we left our country. Then as a girl of ten, the full horror of the events didn't register fully in my young mind. Now as I look back on the time spent in Russia it seems unreal, like a nightmare one can only experience in a dream.

In 1948 all the Polish Refugee Camps in Africa start to liquidate. We said goodbye to father many months ago. He is now in an army camp in England. As usual his letters are very interesting, yet a little depressing. "Once we are released from the army, life will be hard", father writes. "This is a strange country with strange people, strange customs. Worst of all – the English language, with which back in Africa I thought I was sufficiently acquainted, now on many occasions I find utterly frustrating. But we shall be free and the freedom will compensate for the hardship." In one of the letters he tells us that in his spare time from army duties, apart from improving his English, he is learning how to make and repair shoes. Father a cobbler.

Soon we are to leave Africa and go to England. We have a choice; we can go by either sea or air, but mother categorically states that we are sailing. She has never been inside an aeroplane before and has no desire to fly now. "It is extremely dangerous", she said. The thought of departing fills me with great agitation. One part of me is yearning to go and see this island full of ancient traditions and customs, the country I only know from history books and father's letters, yet the other part shrinks from this new, different world. Whenever I think of England, and recently I have been thinking about it a lot, I always have the same mental picture in front of my eyes. I don't see the Houses of Parliament or Westminster Abbey. Instead I see a narrow street made of rows of identical old, brick houses with red roofs and wooden dark doors. One of these houses is ours. Athough several families live on this street and daily we share the same pavement, we hardly know each other. Every family leads its own individual life, arranging their own affairs the way it suits them. No communal camp rules, no one to tell us what we must or mustn't do, and this I think is what I like about my visions. Once the door of our small house is closed, there is only father, mother, Ala and I.

By the time we arrive in England it most probably will be the beginning of winter and father's letters tell us that, even though the grass is always green there and during the last winter only a few snow flakes fell, it gets very damp and windy. As we don't have any winter clothing at all mother buys a huge old cornflower-blue cardigan from someone. Patiently she untangles all the stitches and is now busy knitting jumpers for us. The finished product looks very nice and highly professional. "We will be the smartest girls in town", Ala jokes and, although once again the two jumpers are very much alike, this time Ala doesn't stipulate when I will be allowed to wear mine.

From Mombasa, every couple of months, a large transport of Poles leaves the African shores. It passes through the Red Sea, the Gulf of Suez, the Mediterranean Sea, past the Rock of Gibraltar and up to Southampton in England. Some of my friends left weeks ago, some are staying behind for a little longer. We are leaving tomorrow. The straw hut, our home for many years, now stripped of all the little objects and personal belongings which helped to make it cosy and attractive, looks bare and gloomy. All our worldly possessions are packed into a few wooden boxes and are neatly stacked up inside the door ready to be moved. Our pet, a lovely grey cat, sits on top of them. She looks terribly sad and lonely; I am sure she senses that her comfortable carefree life is changing. I can't bear to think what will happen to her.

It is my last night in Masindi. Tonight it is a full moon. Here in Africa its silver cold light is unusually bright. In the garden I can clearly see the large log of wood propped against a tree, Farasico's favourite sitting place, and tidy rows of tomato plants, father's pride and joy. I gaze up at the star-studded sky trying to spot a shooting star and am suddenly aware that the increasingly loud, familiar tones of the accordion lack their usual cheerfulness. I turn around and, bleary-eyed, look towards a moonlit road. Although Tomek stops playing and looks at me smiling, the lonesome melody lingers on and is in unison with my aching heart. We join hands and silently walk down the narrow, dusty road. All around us the African bushes are burning. The horizon is red from the glare of the fire. The mysterious noises of the jungle, mingled with the tom-tom drums, sound urgent but are as bewitching as my very first night here, six years ago.

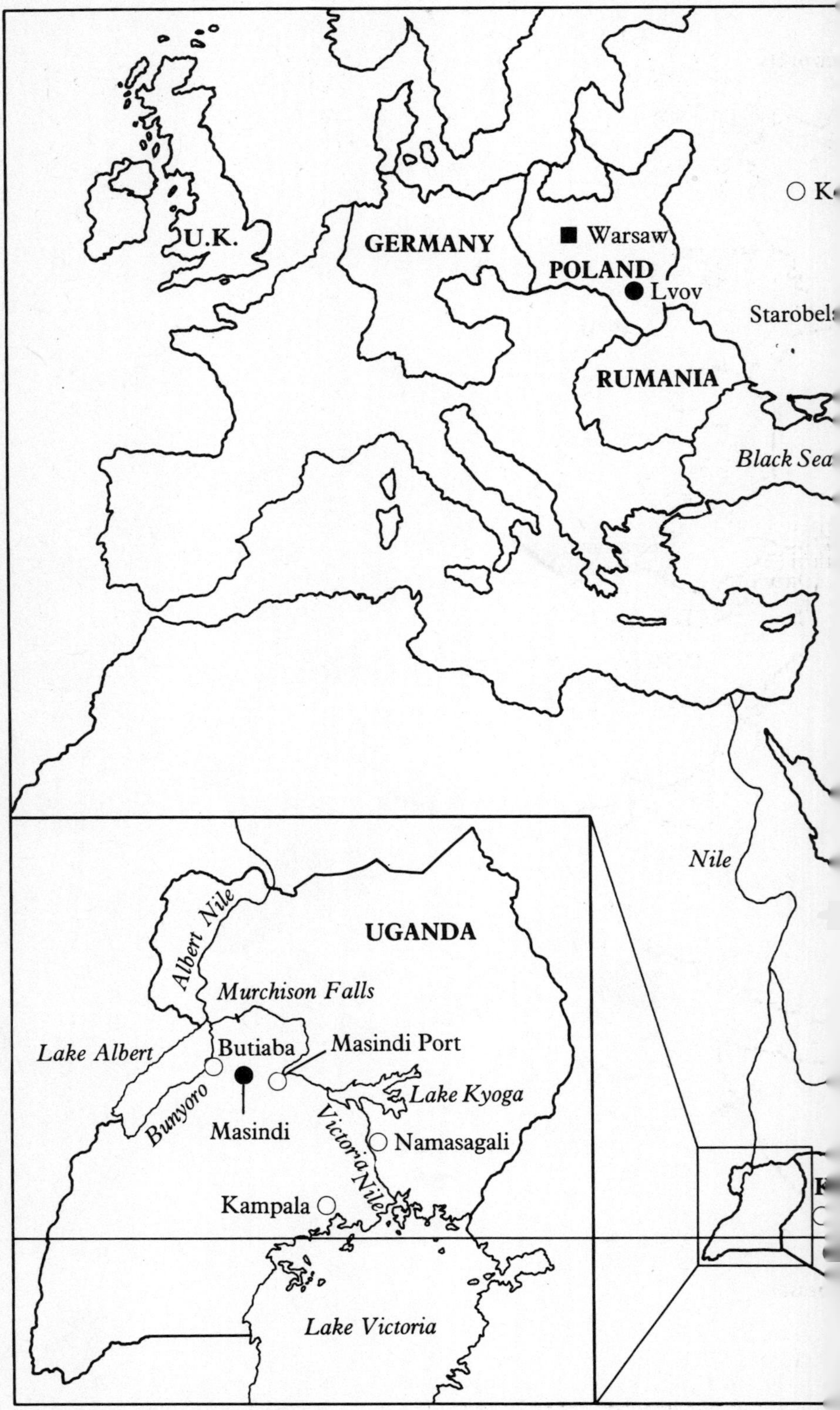

U.K.
GERMANY
Warsaw
POLAND
Lvov
Starobels
RUMANIA
Black Sea
Nile
UGANDA
Albert Nile
Murchison Falls
Lake Albert
Butiaba
Masindi Port
Bunyoro
Masindi
Lake Kyoga
Victoria Nile
Namasagali
Kampala
Lake Victoria